W9-CON-291

AIR MAIL SPECIAL

By BENNY GOODMAN,
JIMMY MUNDY and CHARLIE CHRISTIAN

B♭
F7
B♭
E dim
E dim
F♯dim
Bdim
G♭9
F9
B♭
E♭
E dim
B♭
F9
B♭
E♭
E dim
1. B♭
F7
B♭
2. B♭
F7
B♭

ALRIGHT, OKAY, YOU WIN

Words and Music by SID WYCHE
and MAYME WATTS

Ab9
Eb
Ab7
Eb
Bb+
It's just got-ta be that way.
Well, Al-right,
O-kay,
Eb
Bb+
Eb
Eb7
You Win,
I'm in love with you.
Well, Al-right,
Ab
Eb
O-kay,
You Win,
Ba-by,
Bb7
B7
C7+5
Db7+5
Ab9
what can I do?
An-y-thing you say
I'll do,
As

Eb
Ab7
Eb
Eb6
Ab7
long as it's me and you.
All that I am ask - in',
Eb6
Ab7
Eb6
Ab9
All I want from you,
Just love me like I love you an' it
Eb
Bb7
Tacet
Eb
Bb7
Eb
Bb+
won't be hard to do!
Well, Al - right,
O - kay,
You Win,
Eb
Eb7
Ab
I'm in love with you!
Well, Al - right,
O - kay,
You Win,

Eb
Bb7
B7
C7+5
Db7+5
Ba - by, what can I do?
I'll do an - y - thing you say.
Ba - by, one thing more
If you're gon - na be my man.
Ab9
Eb
Ab7
Eb
It's just got to be that way.
Well, Al - right,
Ab9
Eb
Ab6
Ab9
Eb
Sweet ba - by take me by the hand,
Well, Al - right,
Ab
Eb
Eb
Ab
Eb
Ab
Eb
Eb7
Ab
Fm7-5
Bb7
Bb7+5
Eb9
O - kay, You Win.

ALWAYS TRUE TO YOU IN MY FASHION

from KISS ME, KATE

Words and Music by
COLE PORTER

G7
C
B7sus
4fr
B7
lad more
Yet, to be frank,
Em
Em/D
F♯7/C♯
F♯7♭5/C
B7
Em
C♯dim7
I'd be hap-pier if he had more cash in the bank,
Dm7
G7
G+
C
Dm7
G7
f
Each time we try
C
G7
C
ro - man - tic flights,
He begs for

G7
C
G7
my ex - clu - sive rights,
C
G7
C
My re - ac - tion is to give in. But the ris - in' cost of
F♯m7
B7
Em
Em/D
A7/C♯
Dm7
liv - in' fills my heart with fear, So I
mf
G7
al - ways say to him, "Lis - ten, dear, If a

C
Fmaj7
C
cus - tom tai - lored vet
Asks me out for some - thing wet,
hi - o, Mis - ter Thorne
Calls me up from night 'til morn,
Fm(maj7)
C
C/E
E♭dim7
When the vet be - gins to pet
I cry "Hoo - ray!"
Mis - ter Thorne once cor - nered corn
and that ain't hay,
G7
C/E
E+
But I'm al - ways true to you,
But I'm al - ways true to you,
F6
D♯dim
C/E
Dm7♭5
dar - lin', in my fash - ion,
Yes, I'm
dar - lin', in my fash - ion,
Yes, I'm

C D7 Fm/G G7 C F C/E

al - ways true to you, ___ dar - lin', in my way. ___

al - ways true to you, ___ dar - lin', in my way. ___

E♭dim7 Dm7 Dm7/G C Fmaj7

I've been asked to have a meal ___ By a

From Mil - wau - kee, Mis - ter Fritz ___ Of - ten

p

C Fm(maj7) C

big ty - coon in steel, ___ If the meal in - cludes a deal, ___

dines me at the Ritz, ___ Mis - ter Fritz in - vent - ed Schlitz

C/E E♭dim7 G7

___ ac - cept I may, ___ But I'm

___ And Schlitz must pay! ___ But I'm

C/E E+ F6 D♯dim7 C/E

al - ways true to you, ___ dar - lin', in my fash - ion,
al - ways true to you, ___ dar - lin', in my fash - ion,

Dm7♭5 C D7 Fm/G G7

Yes, I'm al - ways true to you, ___ dar - lin', in my way. _
Yes, I'm al - ways true to you, ___ dar - lin', in my way. _

C F C/E Dm7 C F Fmaj7

There's an oil man known as
Mis - ter Har - ris, plu - to -

F6 Fm C Cmaj7 C6 C7

"Tex" ___ Who is keen to give me checks And his
crat, ___ Wants to give my cheek a pat, If the

F
A7/E
D7
G
checks, I fear, mean that "Tex" is here to stay!
Har - ris pat means a Par - is hat, *Bé - bé!
A7
D7♯5
G7
C/E
F6
D♯dim
C/E
But I'm al - ways true to you, dar - lin', in my fash - ion,
But I'm al - ways true to you, dar - lin', in my fash - ion,
Dm7♭5
C
D7
Fm/G
G7
Yes, I'm al - ways true to you, dar - lin', in my way!
Yes, I'm al - ways true to you, dar - lin', in my way!
1.
C
F
C/E
E♭dim7
Dm7
2.
C
F
C/E
Dm7
C
From O -
f

ANY PLACE I HANG MY HAT IS HOME

from ST. LOUIS WOMAN

Words by JOHNNY MERCER
Music by HAROLD ARLEN

F Gm Fdim Gm F
an - y place I hang my hat is home!
Sweet - nin' wa - ter cher - ry wine,
Bb F
Thank you kind - ly, suits me fine Kan - sas Cit - y,
F+ Db Gm7b5 F
Car - o - line, That's my hon - ey - comb.

B♭7
F
Gm
Fdim
Gm
'Cause an - y place I hang my hat is
F
A♭
G
G♭
Fm
home.
Birds roost - in' in the
D♭
B♭7
tree pick up an' go
An' the go - in'
E♭
C7
Fm
B♭7
proves
That's how it ought to be,
I pick up

D7
A♭m
C7
F
no chord
too When the spir - it moves me.
F
Cross ___ the riv - er 'round the bend, _
How - dy strang - er, so long friend, _ There's a
G7+
C9
G7
Gm7
voice in the lone - some win' ___ that keeps whis - per - in'

F
roam!
I'm go - in'
C7
B♭
E♭m
C7
Fdim
F♯dim
C7
where a wel - come mat is, No mat - ter where that is 'Cause
F
Gm
Fdim
C7
1 F
no chord
F
an - y place I hang my hat is home.
2 F
no chord
F
home.

BEAT ME DADDY, EIGHT TO THE BAR

Words and Music by DON RAYE, HUGHIE PRINCE and ELEANOR SHEEHY

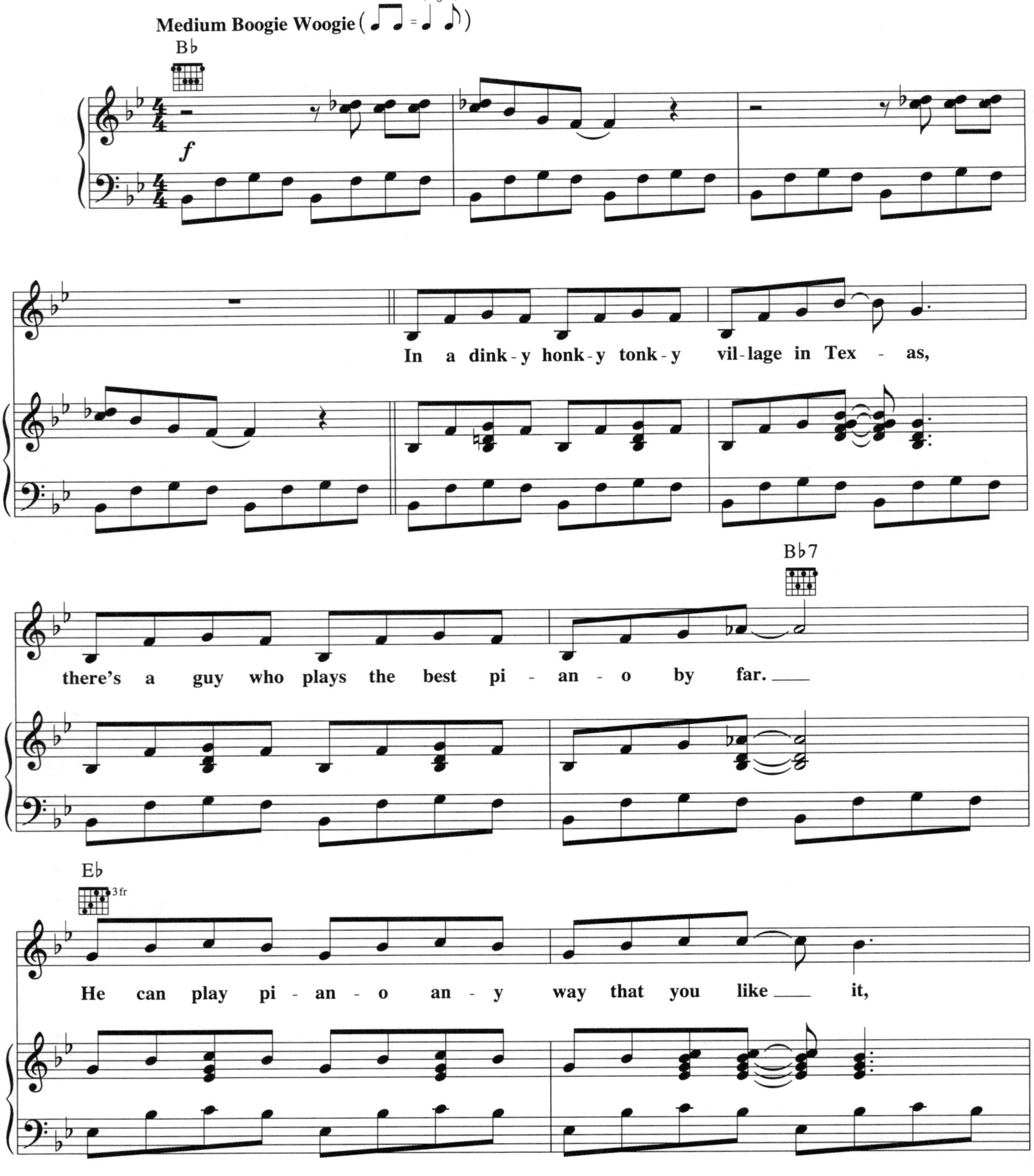

Medium Boogie Woogie

B♭

f

In a dink-y honk-y tonk-y vil-lage in Tex - as,

B♭7

there's a guy who plays the best pi - an - o by far.

E♭ 3fr

He can play pi - an - o an - y way that you like it,

Bb
Bb7
Bdim7
but the style he likes the best is eight to the bar.
F7
When he plays it's a ball, he's the dad - dy of them
Bb
Eb6
Bb
Bb
all.
The peo - ple gath - er a - round when he
Bb7
gets on the stand, then when he plays he gets a hand. The

Eb
3fr
Bb
rhy-thm he beats puts the cats in a trance, no-bod - y there
F7
both - ers to dance. But when he jams with the bass and gui - tar,
Bb
C#dim7
Cm7
3fr
F7
Bb
they hol-ler, "Aw, beat me, dad-dy, eight to the bar." A
plink, a plank, a plink plank plink plank plunk-in' on the keys,

B♭7
E♭
3fr
a riff, a raff, a riff raff riff raff
B♭
riff - in' out with ease.
And when he
F7
jams with the bass and gui - tar,
they hol - ler, "Aw,
B♭
C♯dim7
1
Cm7
F7
B♭
2
Cm7
F7
B♭
beat me, dad - dy, eight to the bar." The peo - ple eight to the bar."

THE BEST THINGS HAPPEN WHILE YOU'RE DANCING

from the Motion Picture Irving Berlin's WHITE CHRISTMAS

Words and Music by
IRVING BERLIN

Cm7
danc - ing
soon be-comes ro - manc - ing
F7
when you hold a girl in your arms that
Cm7/F
F7
F7♯5
B♭maj7
B♭6
you've nev - er held be - fore.
B♭7
B♭dim7
Fm7/B♭
B♭7
E - ven guys with two left feet come

Fm7/B♭
B♭7
Fm7/B♭
B♭7
B♭dim7
out al - right if the girl is sweet, _ if by chance their
Fm7/B♭
B♭7
D7/A
A♭7♭5
G7
Cm9
cheeks should meet _ while danc - ing, _ prov-ing that the
B♭/F
Cm7
F7
1 B♭
D♭dim7
best things hap - pen while _ you dance. _
Cm7
E♭/F
F7
2 B♭
B7♯9(♯11)
B♭6
The dance. _

CHEROKEE
(INDIAN LOVE SONG)

Words and Music by
RAY NOBLE

B♭
Dm
C9
you,
I
can't
for
-
get
Cm7
Fdim
E♭
you,
Cher
-
o
-
kee
sweet
-
F7#5
B♭
F7#5
B♭7
heart.
Child
of
the
prai
-
E♭
E♭m
rie,
your
love
keeps
call
-

B♭
Dm
C9
ing, my heart en - thrall -
Cm7
F7
B♭
ing, Cher - o - kee.
C#m7/F#
F#7
Bmaj7
Dreams of sum - mer - time
B7
Bm7/E
E7
of lov - er - time gone

A
Am7/D
D7
by
throng
my
Gmaj7
G7
Gm7/C
mem - o - ry
so
ten - der - ly
C7
Cm7
F7#5
and
sigh
my
B♭
F7#5
B♭7
sweet
In - dian
maid - en

E♭
E♭m
one day I'll hold you,
B♭
Dm
C9
in my arms fold you,
Cm7
F7
1
B♭
Gm
Cher - o - kee.
R.H.
E♭m/G♭
F7
2
B♭
kee.
R.H.
p

BETWEEN THE DEVIL AND THE DEEP BLUE SEA

from RHYTHMANIA

Lyric by TED KOEHLER
Music by HAROLD ARLEN

Gm7
3fr
C7
F
D♭7
4fr
C7
I sup - pose you'll tell me I'm all wrong.
It's a
F
F7
Dm
B♭m
bit - ter pill to take,
com - ing from you, tho' I've made a big mis - take,
Gm7
C7
F
Gm7
what can I do?
I don't know what makes me string a - long.
F
Gm7
C7
F
I don't want you,
but I'd hate to

Gm7 C7 F7 B♭ B♭m6 F/C Fm6 Gm7 C7

lose you. You've got me in be - tween __ the de - vil and the deep blue sea. __

F C7 F Gm7 C7 F

__ I for - give you, 'cause I can't for -

Gm7 C7 F7 B♭ B♭m6 F/C Fm6/C Gm7 C7

get you. You've got me in be - tween __ the de - vil and the deep blue sea. __

F E7 A6 Bm7 E7

__ I ought to cross you off my list, __

A
Adim
A
F7♯5
E7
Am6
5 fr
C/G
but when you come knock - ing at my door. _
Fate seems to give my
Fm6
A♭7
4 fr
Dm7♭5
G7
C7
F
heart a twist, _ and I come run - ning back for more.
I should
Gm7
3 fr
C7
F
Gm7
3 fr
C7
F7
hate you, but I guess I love you.
You've got me
B♭
B♭m6
6 fr
F/C
Fm6/C
6 fr
Gm7
3 fr
C7
1
F
Cdim7
C7
2
F
in be - tween _ the de - vil and the deep blue sea. ___

BOOGIE WOOGIE BUGLE BOY

from BUCK PRIVATES

Words and Music by DON RAYE
and HUGHIE PRINCE

C
But then his num - ber came up, And he was
G7
gone with the draft. He's in the ar - my now a - blow - in'
F7
C
re - veil - le, He's the Boo - gie Woo - gie Bu - gle Boy of Com - pa - ny B. They
C
made him blow a bu - gle for his Un - cle Sam, It
puts the boys to sleep with "boo - gie" ev - 'ry night, And

C7
real - ly brought him down be - cause he could - n't jam. The cap - tain
wakes them up the same way in the ear - ly bright. They clap their
F
C
seemed to un - der - stand Be - cause the next day the "cap" went out and
hands and stamp their feet Be - cause they know how he plays when some - one
G7
draft - ed a band And now the comp - 'ny jumps
gives him a beat, He real - ly breaks it up
when he plays
F7
C
re - veil - le, He's the Boo - gie Woo - gie Bu - gle Boy of Com - pa - ny B A

toot! A toot! A toot did-dle ah-da toot. He blows it eight to the bar
in "boo-gie" rhy-thm. He can't blow a note un-less a bass and gui-tar is play-in'
with 'im. He makes the comp-'ny jump when he plays
re-veil-le, He's the Boo-gie Woo-gie Bu-gle Boy of Com-pa-ny B. He Com-pa-ny B.
F
C
G7
F7
1
2

BYE BYE BLACKBIRD

from PETE KELLY'S BLUES

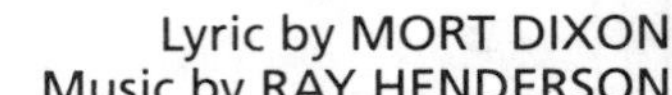

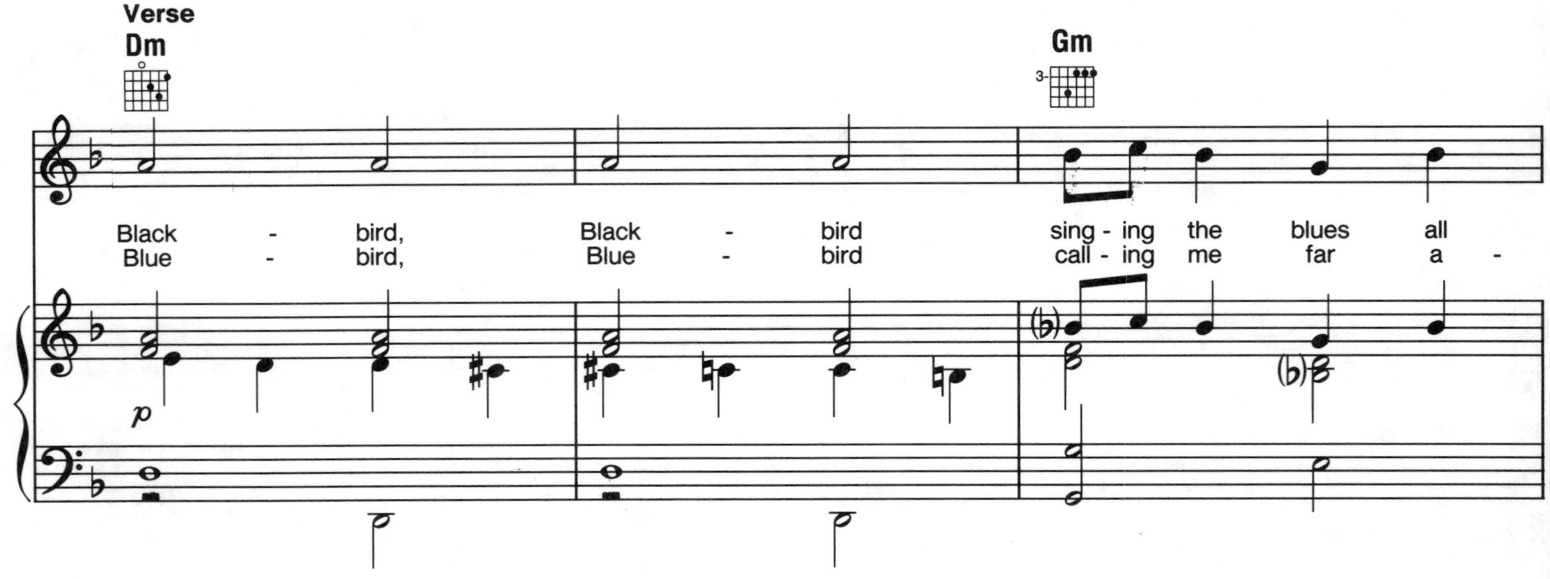

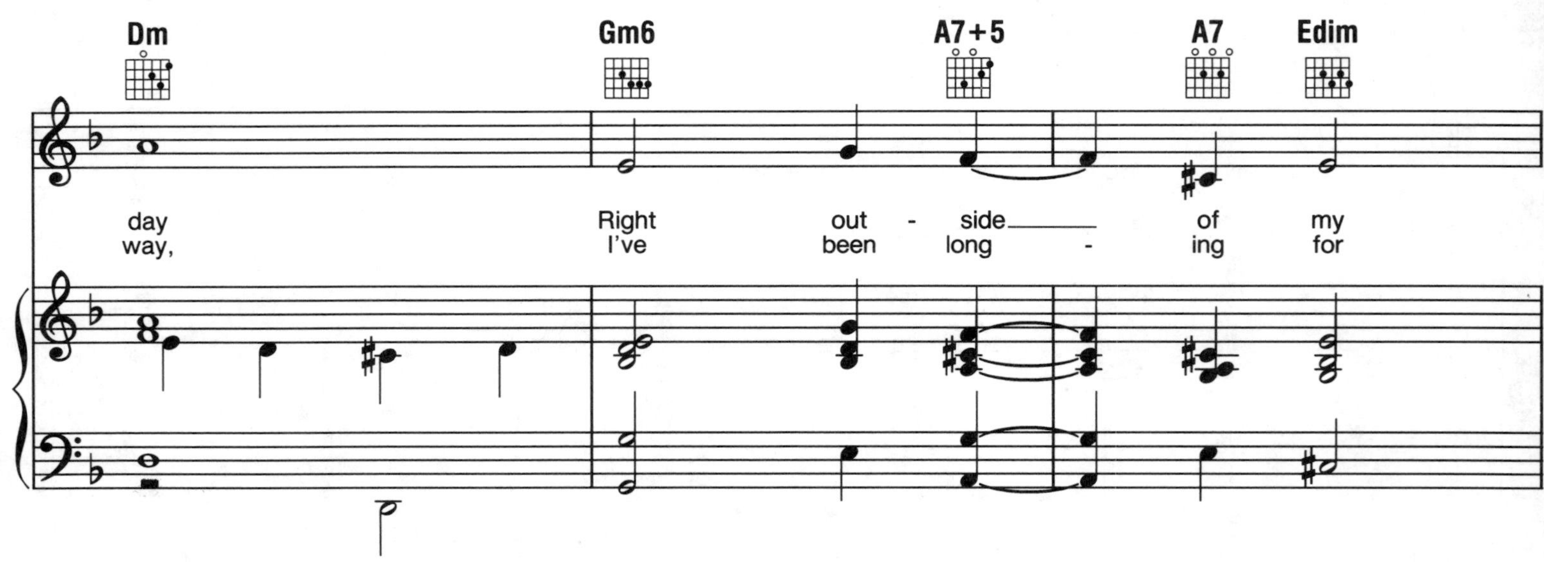

Dm Gm6 Dm A7 A+ A7 Dm

door; Black - bird,
you; Blue - bird,

R.H.

Gm Dm

Black - bird, got - ta be on my way,
Blue - bird, this is my luck - y day,

Dm7 G7 Gm7 B♭m6 C7

Where there's sun - shine ga - lore.
Now my dreams will come true.

Chorus

F F+ Gm Dm F B♭maj7 C9

Pack up all my care and woe, Here I go

p-mf

Am7
F6
F
Fdim
Gm7
C7
sing - ing low, Bye bye black - bird,
Gm
E♭
Am
Gm6
Gm
Where some - bod - y waits for me,
C9
Am
B♭maj7
C9
Gm7
C7
Su - gar's sweet, so is she, Bye bye
Fmaj7
F6
F7
black - bird.
No one here can love and un - der -

Cm6 D7 Gm B♭m6 F G7
stand me, Oh what hard luck sto - ries they all
B♭m6 C7 F F+ Gm Dm F
hand me; Make my bed and light the light,
B♭maj7 C9 Cm6 D7 Gm C7
I'll ar - rive late to - night, black - bird bye
1 F Dm Gm7 C7
bye.
2 F B♭ B♭m6 F6
bye.

CAN'T GET OUT OF THIS MOOD

Words and Music by FRANK LOESSER
and JIMMY McHUGH

(Slowly, with expression)
REFRAIN
C(maj7)
Ebm6
Ab7aug
Ab7
Dm7
CAN'T GET OUT OF THIS MOOD,
Can't get o-ver this
G9
G6
G7
C(maj7)
Ab9
Ebm7
feel-ing,
CAN'T GET OUT OF THIS MOOD,
Last
Dm7
G9
G7
G aug
C6
night, your lips were too ap - peal - ing,
The thrill should have been
Am7
D7
Gm6
A7
B♭m6
A7
all gone by to - day,
In the us - u-al

D7
C
Dm7(b5)
D7
Abm6
G7
C
G7
way, But it's on - ly your arms I'm
F#dim
Dm7
G7
C(maj7)
Ebm6
Ab7 aug
Ab7
out of; Can't get out of this dream,
poco rit.
Dm7
G9
G6
G7
C(maj7)
Ab9
What a fool to dream of you; 'Twas-n't part of my scheme,
Ebm7
Dm7
G#dim
E7
To sigh and tell you that I love you, But

E7
Am
Am7
D7
Gm6
I'm say - ing it, I'm play - ing it dumb,
A
A9
Ab9
Ab7aug
Ab7
Dm7
CAN'T GET OUT OF THIS MOOD,
Heart - break,
cresc. molto
1.
D7(b5)
G(7)
C
Db
Dm7
Bdim
Abm6
Here I come!
mf
mp
2.
Ab9
G9
C
Em
Ebm
C(maj7)
Here I come!
l.h.
l.h.
mf
f

CIRIBIRIBIN

Based on the original melody by A. PESTALOZZA
English Version by HARRY JAMES and JACK LAWRENCE

F6 Gm7 Ab dim F6/A F6
Ci-ri-bi-ri-bin She throws a rose and
F+ Bb D7/A D7-5/Ab Gm
blows a kiss from up a-bove Ci-ri-bi-ri-
Gm7 Dm/A Bb7 Bb7 Db/B F/C Gdim
bin, Ci-ri-bi-ri-bin, Ci-ri-bi-ri-bin They're
C7 1. F6 Ab dim C7 2. F6 Eb7 F6 C9+ F6
so in love. Ci-ri-bi-ri- love.

DON'T GET AROUND MUCH ANYMORE

Words and Music by BOB RUSSELL
and DUKE ELLINGTON

G7
C
F
Fm
C
Don't Get A - round Much An - y More
Dar - ling I guess my minds
C7+5
F
F♯dim
G7
F♯dim
G7
more at ease but nev - er - the - less
why stir up mem - o - ries
C
A7
Been in - vit - ed on dates
Might have gone but what for
Am7
D7
G7
1 C
Aw - f'lly dif - f'rent with - out you
Don't Get A - round Much An - y More
2 C
C7(♯9)
Missed the Sat - ur - day More.

DON'T SIT UNDER THE APPLE TREE
(WITH ANYONE ELSE BUT ME)

Words and Music by LEW BROWN,
SAM H. STEPT and CHARLIE TOBIAS

Chorus, Brightly
F
C7
D7
Gm7
Cm6
G7
B♭
mp
Don't Sit Un-der The Ap-ple Tree with an-y-one else but me,
An-y-one else but me, An-y-one else but me, No! No! No!
Just re-mem-ber that I've been true to no-bod-y else but you, So
just be true to me.

F
C7
F
D7
Don't go walk-ing down lov - ers' lane with an - y - one else but me,
Gm7
C7
Gm7
C7
F
Gm7
C7
F
C7
Gm7
C7
An - y - one else but me, An - y - one else but me, No! No! No!
F
C7
F
Cm6
D7
Don't start show-ing off all your charms in some-bod - y else'- s arms, You
G7
Gm7
C7
F
Gm7
F
F7
B♭
must be true to me. I'm so a - fraid that the
mf

Gm7
C9
F
C7
F
A7
Dm
Dm7
plans we made un-der-neath those moon-lit skies Will fade a-way and you're
Dm6
G9
C7
Dm7
Cdim
C7
C7 aug
F
C7
bound to stray if the stars get in your eyes, So, Don't Sit Un-der The
F
F
Cm6
D7
G7
Ap-ple Tree with an-y-one else but me, You're my L-
Gm7
C7
1. F
Bb
F
Cdim
Gm7
C7
2. F
Bb6
F
O-V-E.
E.

DROP ME OFF IN HARLEM

Words by NICK KENNY
Music by DUKE ELLINGTON

Eb Cm7 F13 Bb Bdim7 Cm7 F7
Heav-en up in Har-lem. I don't want your Dix - ie,
Ddim7 Dbm6 Cm7 F7 Cm Cm/Eb Bb/F F#dim7
you can keep your Dix - ie. There's no one down in
Gm7 Fm Bb7 Eb Cm7 F13 Bb
Dix - ie who can take me 'way from my own Har - lem.
Bb7 Bb7#5 Eb Bb7#5 Eb9
Har-lem has those south-ern skies, they're in my ba-by's smile, I

A♭7
D♭7
C7
F13
i - dol - ize my ba-by's eyes and class - y up - town style. If
B♭6
Bdim7
Cm7
F7
Ddim7
D♭m6
Har-lem moved to Chi - na, I know of noth - ing fin -
Cm7
F7
Cm
Cm/E♭
B♭/F
F♯dim7
Gm7
Fm
B♭7
- er, than to stow - a - way on a 'plane some day and have them
E♭
Cm7
F13
1 B♭
2 B♭
drop me off in Har - lem.
Har - lem.
fz

FIVE GUYS NAMED MOE

Words and Music by LARRY WYNN
and JERRY BRESLER

F6
D7
four eyed
Moe,
(fill)
F6
D7
no Moe,
(fill)
Dm6
G9
look at bro - ther,
look at bro - ther,
Gm9
C7
look at bro - ther eat Moe,

Moe.
Moe.
Moe.
Moe.
Moe.
F
F#°
Gm7
G#°
Am7
A♭°
Gm7
Gm7/C
Who's the great - est band a - round, makes the cats jump up and down,
F
F7/A
B♭
B°
B♭/C
who's the talk of rhy-thm town, five guys named Moe, that's us.
F
F#°
Gm7
G#°
Am7
A♭°
Gm7
C7
When they start to beat it out, ev - 'ry-bo - dy jumps and shouts,

F
F7/A
B♭
B°
B♭/C
tell me who the cri - tics all rave a - bout five guys named Moe, Ah!
F7
We came out of no - where that don't mean a thing.
G7
N.C./C
to Coda
Fm/C
We rate high and you'll know why when you hear us sing,
E♭/C
Fm/C
Cm
sing, sing, sing, sing.

F
F♯°
Gm7
G♯°
F/A
A♭°
Gm7
C7
High brow, low brow, they all a - gree
we're the best in har - mo - ny
I'm
F
F7/A
B♭
B°
B♭/C
D.𝄋 al Coda
tell - ing you folks, you real - ly ought to see five guys named Moe.
CODA
C♭/D♭
sing.

G♭
G°
A♭m7
A°
B♭m7
A°
A♭m7
D♭7
We're the great - est band a - round,
makes the cats jump up and down,
G♭
G♭7/B♭
C♭
C°
D♭
we're the talk of rhy-thm town,
five guys named Moe.
Not
A♭9
one guy,
(No Moe)
not
A9
two guys,
(Little Biddy Moe)
not
(ad lib. fill)

B♭9
three guys,
(Four Eyed Moe)
not
(fill)
C♭9
four guys,
(Big Moe)
but
five guys,
C9
(fill)
(Eat Moe)
Cm9
F6/7
five lit - tle guys named
(fill)
B♭6/9
B♭
Moe,
Moe,
Moe,
Moe,
Moe,
that's us.

EVERYBODY LOVES MY BABY
(BUT MY BABY DON'T LOVE NOBODY BUT ME)

Words and Music by JACK PALMER
and SPENCER WILLIAMS

With a beat

VERSE

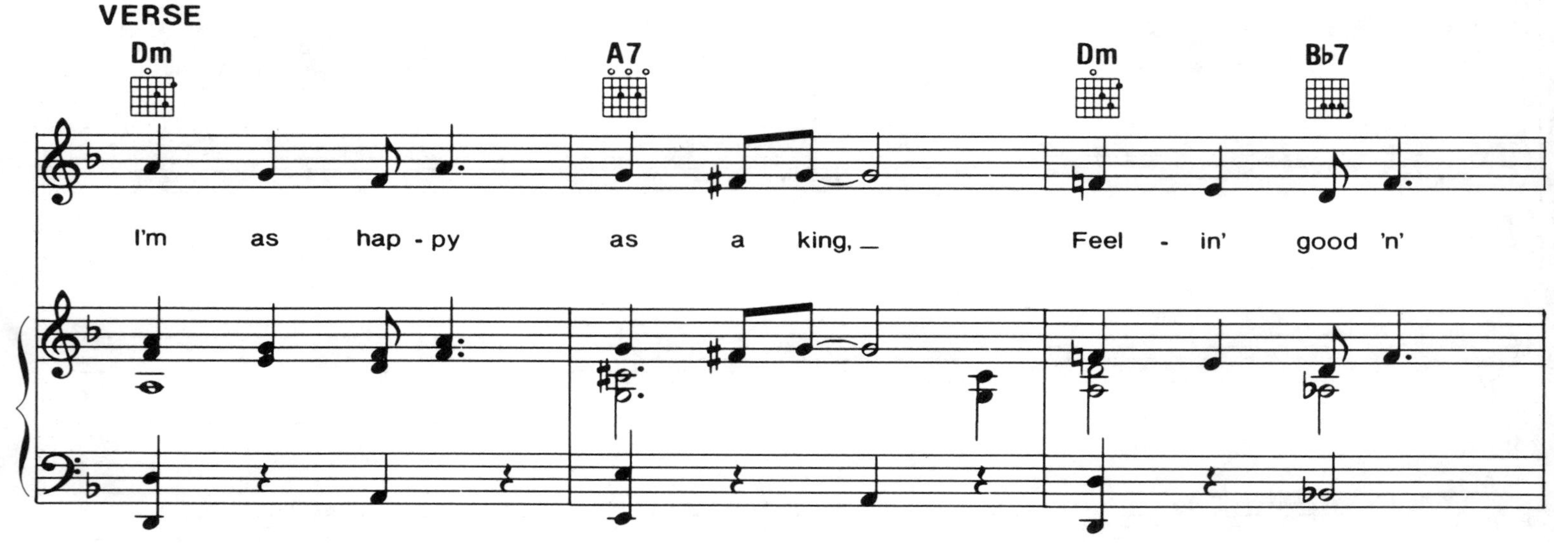

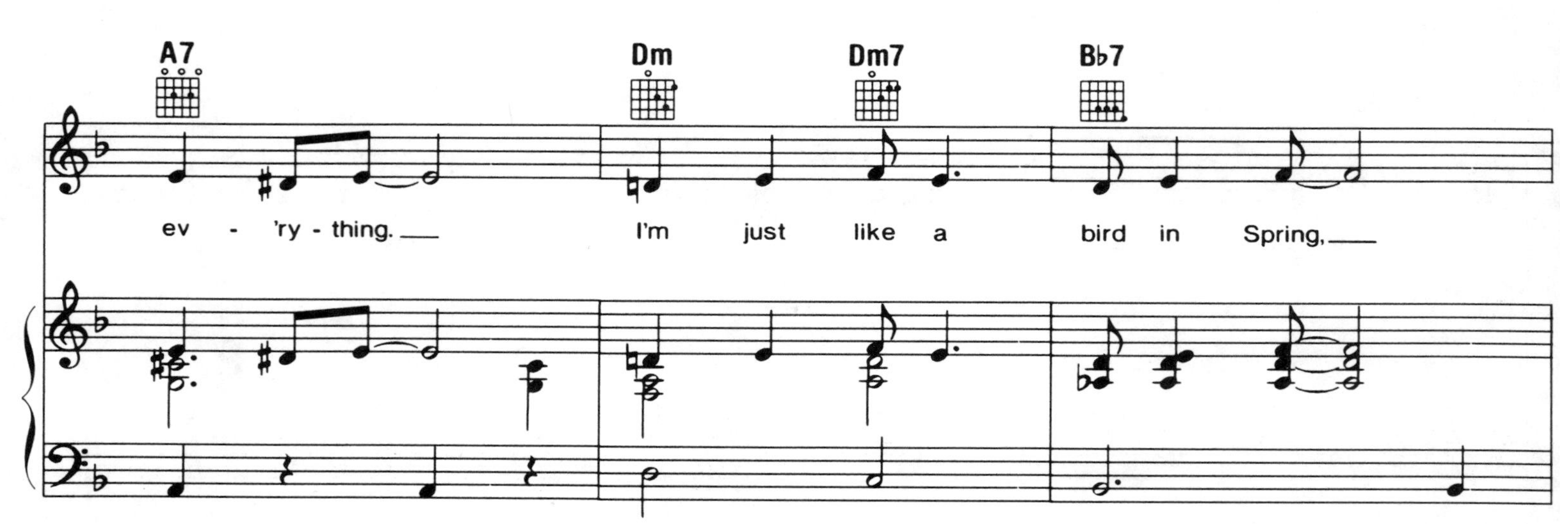

Dm Bb7 A7 Dm A7
Got to let it out. It's my sweet-ie, can't you guess?
Dm Bb7 A7 Dm Dm7 Bb7
Wild a-bout her, I'll con-fess; Does she love me? Oh, my, yes!
Dm Bb7 A7 Em7 A7 Dm
That's just why I shout: Ev-'ry-bod-y loves my ba-by
G7 C7 C+
But my ba-by don't love no-bod-y but me, No-bod-y but

F6
A7
Dm
me.
Ev - 'ry - bod - y wants my ba - by,
But my ba - by don't want no - bod - y but me,
A
B♭dim
E7
That's plain to
A
A♭dim
C7
F7
Fdim
F7
Fdim
F7
see.
I am his sweet Pa - too - tie and he
She is my
I
Now when my ba - by kiss - es me up -
Say
She's got a form like Ve - nus, hon - est,
Fdim
F7
B♭
F+
is my lov - in' man, Knows how to do his
am her
her
on my ros - y cheeks, I just let those
I ain't talk - ing Greek, No one can come be -

Bb
G7
C7
A7
du - ty, Loves_ me like no oth - er can.
kiss - es be, ___ Don't wash my face for weeks.
tween us, She's_ my She - ba, I'm her Sheik.
That's why
Dm
ev - 'ry - bod - y loves my ba - by, But my ba - by don't
G7
C7
love no - bod - y but me. ___
No - bod - y but
1,2
F
Bb9
A7
me.
3
F
me. ___

FLAT FOOT FLOOGIE

Words and Music by SLIM GAILLARD,
SLAM STEWART and BUD GREEN

* Pronounced so as to rhyme with "HOW"

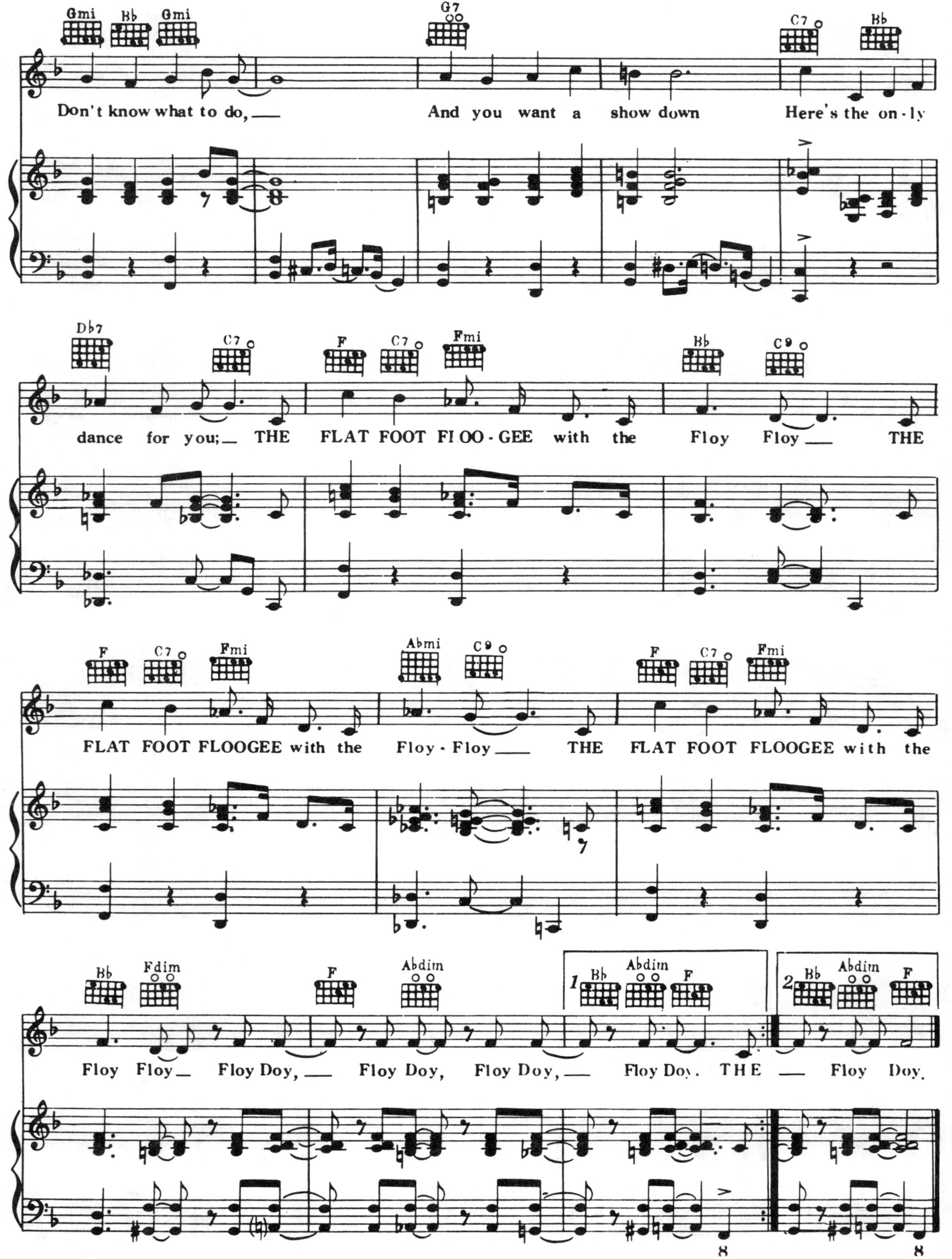
Gmi
Bb
Gmi
G7
C7
Bb
Don't know what to do, __ And you want a show down Here's the on-ly
Db7
C7
F
C7
Fmi
Bb
C9
dance for you; __ THE FLAT FOOT FLOO-GEE with the Floy Floy __ THE
F
C7
Fmi
Abmi
C9
F
C7
Fmi
FLAT FOOT FLOOGEE with the Floy-Floy __ THE FLAT FOOT FLOOGEE with the
Bb
Fdim
F
Abdim
Bb
Abdim
F
Bb
Abdim
F
Floy Floy __ Floy Doy, __ Floy Doy, Floy Doy, __ Floy Doy. THE __ Floy Doy.

FLYING HOME

Music by BENNY GOODMAN and LIONEL HAMPTON
Lyric by SID ROBIN

A♭
A♭7/G♭
Fm
E9
E♭9
flying home to my little home-town honey
A♭
E♭m6
A♭9
A9
waitin' for me there.
A♭
A♭7/G♭
Fm
E9
E♭9
C'mon let's go, don't you mind this sudden flurry?
A♭
A♭7/G♭
Fm
E9
E♭9
Don't you know that I'm in an awful hurry?

Ab
Ab7/Gb
Fm
E9
Eb9
Ain't it so
that my ba - by's gon - na wor - ry
Ab
Ebm6
Ab
if I don't get
there?
My
heart is burn - in' ev - er since I've been learn - in' how I
Db
missed { her, him, }
since I kissed { her. him. }
Now

B♭7
A7
I can't stand it, won't you please un - der - stand that I've been
E♭7
E♭dim7
E♭7
lone - some, I've been liv - ing by my own - some.
A♭
A♭7/G♭
Fm
E9
E♭9
Fly - ing home, from now on there's no more griev - in'.
A♭
A♭7/G♭
Fm
E9
E♭9
I won't roam, once I'm there I'm nev - er leav - in'.

A♭
A♭7/G♭
Fm
E9
E♭9
Fly - ing home, _ to that love I'll be re - ciev - in'.
A♭
E♭m6
A♭7
E♭7
A♭
We'll be so hap - py; that's why I'm fly - ing home. _
1
no chord
E9
E♭9
2
A7♭5
A♭

GOT A DATE WITH AN ANGEL

from FOR THE LOVE OF MIKE

Words by CLIFFORD GREY and SONNY MILLER
Music by JACK WALLER and JOSEPH TURNBRIDGE

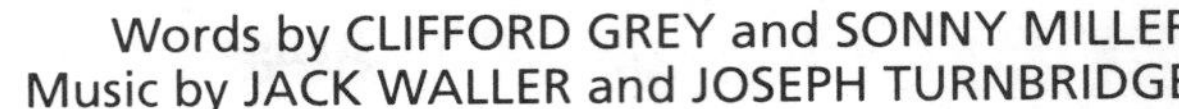

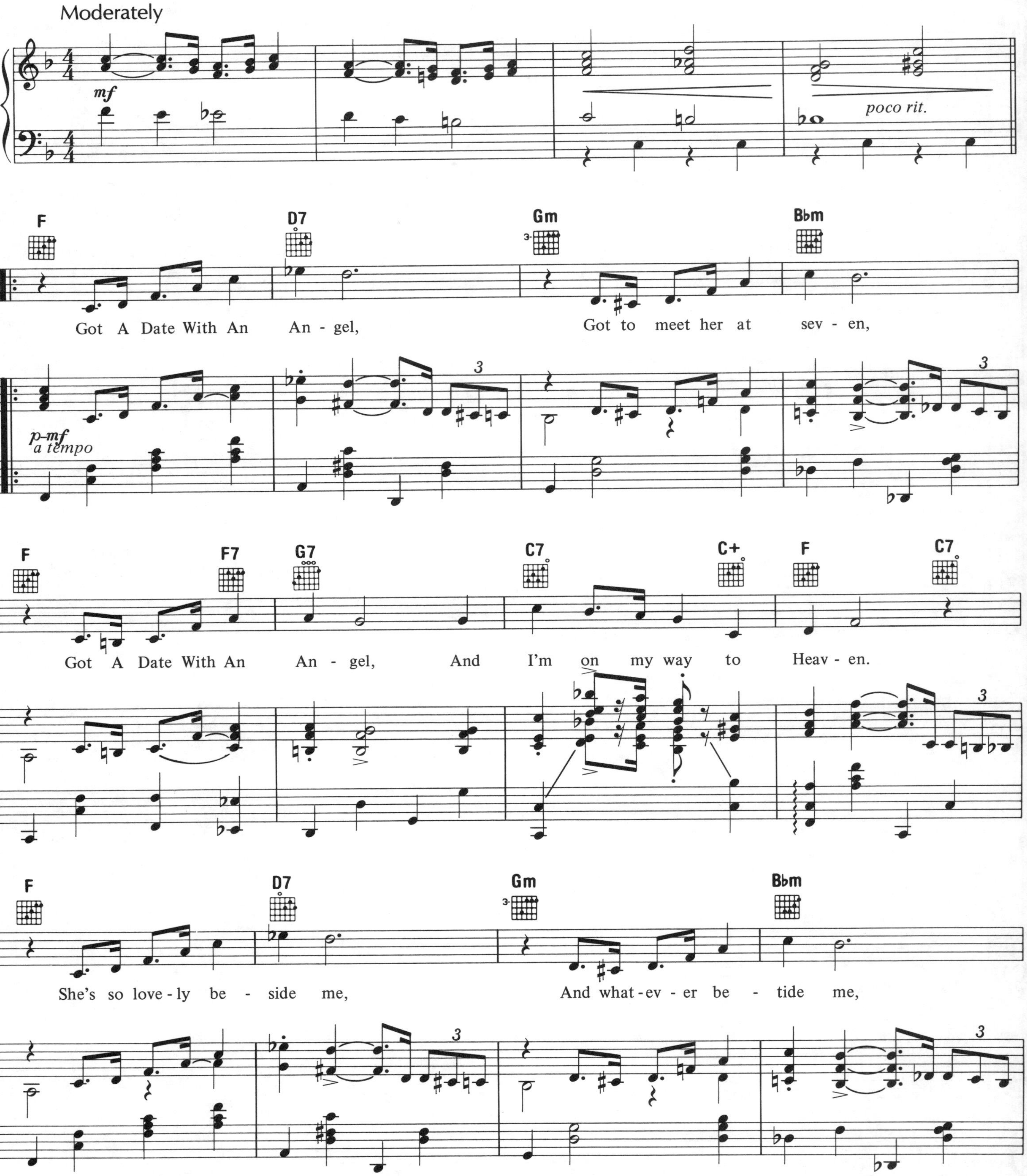

Moderately
mf
poco rit.
F
D7
Gm
Bbm
Got A Date With An An - gel, Got to meet her at sev - en,
p-mf
a tempo
F
F7
G7
C7
C+
F
C7
Got A Date With An An - gel, And I'm on my way to Heav - en.
F
D7
Gm
Bbm
She's so love - ly be - side me, And what - ev - er be - tide me,

F
F7
G7
C7
C+
F
F+
Got an an-gel to guide me, So I'm on my way to Heav-en.
Bb
A
D7
G
Soon I'll hear the bells ring out, And the cho-ir will sing out,
mf
C7
F
A7
D7
G7
Gm
C7
F
When the pearl-y gates swing out She'll beck-on to me. I've been wait-ing a
p
D7
Gm
Bbm
F
F7
life - time, For this eve-ning at sev - en, Got A Date With An
G7
C7
C+
F
C+
F
An - gel And I'm on my way to Heav - en. Heav - en.
f

HONEYSUCKLE ROSE

from AIN'T MISBEHAVIN'

Words by ANDY RAZAF
Music by THOMAS "FATS" WALLER

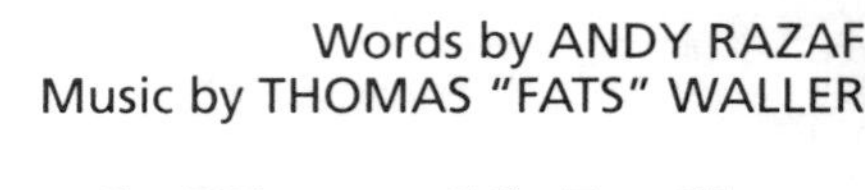

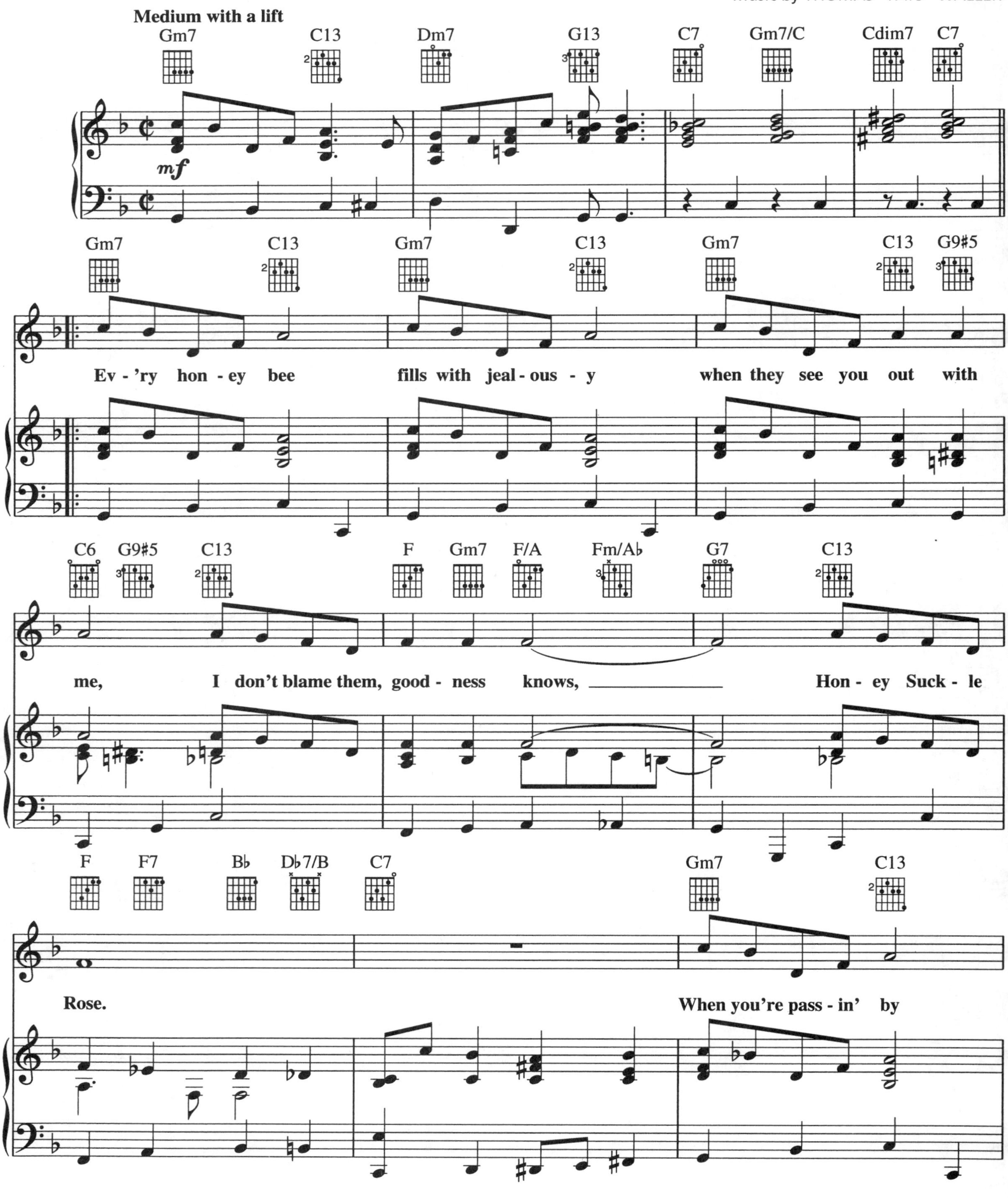

Medium with a lift
Gm7 C13 Dm7 G13 C7 Gm7/C Cdim7 C7
mf
Gm7 C13 Gm7 C13 Gm7 C13 G9♯5
Ev - 'ry hon - ey bee fills with jeal - ous - y when they see you out with
C6 G9♯5 C13 F Gm7 F/A Fm/A♭ G7 C13
me, I don't blame them, good - ness knows, Hon - ey Suck - le
F F7 B♭ D♭7/B C7 Gm7 C13
Rose. When you're pass - in' by

Gm7
C13
Gm7
C13
G9♯5
C6
G9♯5
C13
flow - ers droop and sigh,
and I know the rea - son why.
You're much sweet-er,
F
Gm7
F/A
Fm/A♭
G7
C13
F
F/C
Ddim
C7/E
F
good - ness knows,
Hon - ey Suck - le Rose.
F7
Cm7/F
Fdim7
F7
B♭
F9
G♭9
F9
B♭6
Don't buy sug - ar,
you just have to touch my cup.
G7
Dm7/G
Gdim7
G7
C7
Gm7
You're my sug - ar,
it's sweet when you

A♭9
G9
C7
Gm7
C13
Gm7
C13
stir it up. __ When I'm tak - in' sips from your tas - ty lips,
Gm7
C13
G9♯5
C6
G9♯5
C13
F
Gm7
F/A
Fm/A♭
seems the hon - ey fair - ly drips. You're con - fec - tion, good - ness knows, __
G7
C13
1
F
B♭6/9
D♭7
F/C
A♭dim7
__ Hon - ey Suck - le Rose. __
2
F
F7
Bdim
B♭m
F
Rose. __
3
3
3

HIT THE ROAD TO DREAMLAND

from the Paramount Picture STAR SPANGLED RHYTHM

Words by JOHNNY MERCER
Music by HAROLD ARLEN

Moderato

mf rit.

F7 Bb F+ Bb9 F+ Bb

Voice rubato

Twin-kle, twin-kle, twin-kle, twin-kle goes the star, Twin-kle, twin-kle, twin-kle, twin-kle

mp rubato

F+ Bb9 F7 Bb F+ Bb9 F7 Bb9

there you are. Time for all good child - ren to hit the hay.

Fm7 Bb+ Eb Ebm D+ G9

Cock-a-doo-dle, doo-dle, doo-dle broth-er it's an - oth- er day

r.h.

Gm7
F♯dim
C7
E♭
F7
Adim
We should be on our way!
rit.
B♭
Refrain Moderato
Gm
Cm7
Bye, bye, ba - by Time to hit the road to dream - land You're my
mp - mf
F7
F9
F+
ba - by Dig you in the land of Nod. Hold tight ba - by
We'll be swing - ing up in dream - land All night ba - by
F
D7
D+
C
Fm
D9
where the lit - tle Cher - ubs trod. Look at that knocked out moon, Been a blow -
cresc. poco - a - poco

D9-5
Am7
D9
Dm7
G7
Dm7
G7
- in' his top in the blue
Nev- er saw the likes of
mf - f
Eb
F7
Bb
you;
What an An- gel. Bye, bye, ba - by
Gm
Cm7
F7
Time to hit the road to dream - land. Don't cry ba - by
Cm7
F+9
Dm7
Gm
F#dim
Gm7
Ab9-5
G9
Cm7
It was di- vine but the roost- er has fin-'lly crowed
Time to hit the
cresc. poco a poco
mf - f
Bb
Gm
C7
F7
Bb
Gm
C7
F7
Bb
F+
Bb9
road.
road.
rit.

I GOT THE SUN IN THE MORNING

from the Stage Production ANNIE GET YOUR GUN

Words and Music by
IRVING BERLIN

Light bounce

C9/B♭ C9 C6/9 Gm7

mf

C9 F6 E♭6

Tak - ing stock_ of what I have_ and what I

F6 C9 C9♯5 F Dm7

have - n't, ___ what do I find?__ The things I've got will

G7 C7 F6 Gm7 F6

keep me sat - is - fied. ___

A♭6
G♭6
A♭6
Check-ing up on what I have and what I have - n't,
Adim
C/G
A7
Dm7
G7
C7
what do I find? A health - y bal - lance on the cred - it side.
Medium jump tempo
C7♭5/G♭
F6
Got no dia - mond,
C7♭5/G♭
F6
C7♭5/G♭
F6
F7
got no pearl, still I think I'm a luck - y girl. I got the

B♭ F/A Gm7 F6 B♭ F
sun in the morn-ing and the moon at night.
Gm7 F6 C7♭5/G♭ F6 C7♭5/G♭ F6
Got no man - sion, got no yacht,
C7♭5/G♭ F6 F7 B♭ F/A
still I'm hap - py with what I've got. I got the sun in the morn-ing and the
Gm7 F6 B♭ F Gm7 F6
moon at night.

A7
D7sus
Sun - shine gives me a love - ly day.
D9
G7
B♭maj7/C
Moon - light gives me the milk - y way.
C9
C7♭5/G♭
F6
Got no check - books,
C7♭5/G♭
F6
C7♭5/G♭
F6
got no banks, still I'd like to ex -

F7 B♭ F/A
press my thanks. I got the sun in the morn-ing and the
Gm7 F6 B♭ F
moon at night.
Gm7 F6 F7 B♭ F/A A♭dim Gm7
And with the sun in the morn-ing and the moon in the eve-ning, I'm
C7♭9 F6 1 C7 2 G♭7 F
all right.

I HEAR MUSIC

from the Paramount Picture DANCING ON A DIME

F/C C7 F Am Am7/G

mu - sic in my soul. Not that I'm a

F♯m7♭5 4fr F7 E7 Am Am7/G

Pol - ly - an - na, shout - in' out a

F♯m7♭5 4fr F7 E7 Am Am7/G

loud ho - zan - na. It's my sing - ing

F♯m7♭5 4fr G7 C7

heart I can't con - trol.

Am7♭5
D+
G7
C7
I hear mu - sic, might - y fine
mu - sic, the mur - mur of a morn - ing breeze up there, the
F7
B♭
rat - tle of the milk - man on the stair.
F
Sure that's
mu - sic, might - y fine mu - sic, the

F7
B♭
F7
B♭
C7
F
sing - ing of a spar - row in the sky, the perk - ing of the cof - fee
C7
F
Cm7
3 fr
F9
Cm7
3 fr
F9
right near - by. There's my fa - v'rite
B♭maj7
B♭6
B♭maj7
B♭6
B♭m7
E♭9
mel - o - dy, You, my
B♭m7
E♭7
A♭
4fr
Gm7
3fr
C7
an - gel, phon - ing me.

Am7♭5
D+
G7
C7
Am7♭5
D+
I hear mu - sic, mighty - y fine
G7
C7
F7
B♭
F7
B♭
mu - sic, and an - y-time I think my world is wrong, I
C7
F
Gm7
3 fr
Gm7/C
C7
1 F
get me out of bed and sing this song.
Gm7
3 fr
C7
2 F
Gm7
3 fr
G♭9
3 fr
Fmaj7
song.

I LET A SONG GO OUT OF MY HEART

Words and Music by DUKE ELLINGTON, HENRY NEMO,
JOHN REDMOND and IRVING MILLS

Eb
Ab
Eb
Cm7
I let a song go out of my heart,
C7
it was the sweet - est mel - o - dy.
Ab6
Cm/G
Fm7
F#dim7
Eb/G
Ab
I know I lost heav - en 'cause
Eb
Cm7
Fm7b5
Bb7
Eb
Ab
you were the song.
Since you and I have

E♭ 3fr
Cm7 3fr
C7
drift - ed a - part life does - n't mean a thing to me. __
A♭6 3fr
Cm/G 3fr
Fm7
F♯dim7
E♭/G 3fr
A♭ 4fr
E♭ 3fr
A♭m 4fr
Please come back, _ sweet mu - sic, ______ I know I was wrong. ______
E♭ 3fr
E♭/G 3fr
F♯dim
Fm7
Fm7♭5
B♭7
__ Am I too late ______ to make a -
E♭ 3fr
E♭maj7 3fr
E♭6
E♭/G 3fr
A♭ 4fr
G7
Cm 3fr
Cm7 3fr
mends? ______ You know that we were meant to

G♭9
B7
B♭9
B♭9♯5
be more than just friends,
just friends.
E♭
A♭
E♭
Cm7
C7
I let a song go out of my heart.
Be - lieve me, dar-ling,
A♭6
Cm/G
Fm7
F♯dim7
E♭/G
A♭
when I say I won't know sweet mu - sic un -
E♭
B♭7♭9
1
E♭6
B♭7
2
E♭6
A♭m6
E♭
til you re-turn some - day.
day.
rit.

I THOUGHT ABOUT YOU

Words by JOHNNY MERCER
Music by JIMMY VAN HEUSEN

Fm7
Bb13
5fr
Eb
3fr
D7
What did I find?
I took a trip on the train
Db9b5
C9
F9
Cm7
3fr
F7
and I thought a-bout you.
3
Fm7
Bb
G7
Cm
3fr
I passed a shad-ow-y lane
and I thought a-bout you.
3
Bbm7
Eb13
5fr
Ab
4fr
Abm6
4fr
Two or three cars parked un-der the stars, a

Eb/Bb
6fr
Bb/Ab
Gm7
3fr
Cm7
3fr
D7sus
D7
wind - ing stream,
moon shin-ing down on
D7sus
D7
Gm
3fr
Edim7
Fm7
Bb7
some lit-tle town, and with each beam, same old dream.
Eb
3fr
D7
Db9b5
C9
F9
At ev - 'ry stop that me made, oh, I thought a-bout you.
Cm7
3fr
F7
Fm7
Bb
G7
But when I pulled down the shade, then I

Cm
3fr
Bbm7
Eb7
Ab
4fr
Ab6
3fr
real - ly felt blue.
I peeked thru the crack and
3
Abm6
4fr
Eb
3fr
Eb6
Ab9
4fr
F9
F#dim7
looked at the track,
the one go-ing back
to you.
And
1
Fm7
Bb13
5fr
Fm7
Bb7b9
Eb6
Cm
3fr
what did I do?
I thought a-bout you!
Fm7
Fm9/Bb
Bb7
2
Eb6
E7#9
Eb6
3
3
3

I WON'T DANCE

from ROBERTA

Lyrics by OSCAR HAMMERSTEIN II and OTTO HARBACH
Screen Version by DOROTHY FIELDS and JIMMY McHUGH
Music by JEROME KERN

Dm C Dm7 G7 Em Dm G7
So ec - sta - tic - 'lly You just look and say em - pha - tic - 'lly
C Cmaj7 Dm7 G7 C Cmaj7 Dm7 G7
Not this sea - son! There's a rea - son!
mf
Refrain
C Em Dm F G7 C Em
He: I won't dance! Don't ask me; I won't dance!
p
Dm F G7 C Em Dm F G7
Don't ask me; I won't dance, Ma - dame, with

C
Cmaj7
C7
B♭
Fmaj7
F6
Fm
G7
C
you.
My heart won't let my feet do things they should do!
Dm7
G7
C
Cmaj7
You know what?
Dm7
G7
C
Cmaj7
Dm7
G7
C
Cmaj7
You're love - ly, She: And so what? I'm love - ly! He: But oh! What
Dm7
G7
C
Cmaj7
C7
Gm7
Fmaj7
F6
you do to me!
I'm like an o - cean wave that's

Fm
G7
C
B♭
C
F
Fmaj7
F6
bumped on the shore;
I feel so ab - so - lute - ly
mf
Fm
G7
C
C6
Dm7
G7
stumped on the floor!
A♭
A♭7
She: When you dance you're charm - ing and you're gen - tle!
mp
D♭
'Spec - 'lly when you do the "Con - ti -

D♭7
B
-nen - tal." He: But this feel - ing
B7
C7
B♭
is - n't pure - ly men - tal; For heav - en
E7
Am
Dm
F
rest us, I'm not as - bes - tos.
G7
C
Em
Dm
F
G7
And that's why I won't dance! Why should I?
mp

C
Em
Dm
F
G7
C
Em
I won't dance!
How could I?
I won't dance!
Dm
F
G7
C
Cmaj7
C7
Gm7
Fmaj7
F6
Mer - ci beau - coup!
I know that mu - sic leads the
Fmaj7
G7
C
C7
Gm7
Fmaj7
B♭6
A
A♭7
way to ro - mance:
So if I hold you in my
Fmaj7
G7
C
Gdim
F
A♭7
arms I won't dance!
8va
p
8va
sf

I'M BEGINNING TO SEE THE LIGHT

Words and Music by DON GEORGE, JOHNNY HODGES,
DUKE ELLINGTON and HARRY JAMES

G6
E♭7
D7
G
G6
E♭7
D7
nev - er went in for af - ter glow, Or can - dle - light on the
E♭7
G6
D7
G
Dm
E7
mis - tle - toe, But now when you turn the lamp down low I'm be -
A7
Am7
D7
G
B7
gin - ning to see the light. Used to ram - ble
B♭7
thru the park Shad - ow box - ing in the dark

A7
E♭7
Then you came and caused a spark, That's a four a - larm fire now.
Am7
D7
G6
E♭7
D7
G
I nev - er made love by lan - tern shine, I
E♭7
D7
E♭7
G
D7
nev - er saw rain - bows in my wine, But now that your lips are
G
Dm
E7
A7
Am7
D7
1 G
Gdim
D9
2 G
D7+5
G
burn-ing mine, I'm be - gin-ning to see the light. I
8vb

I'VE GOT YOU UNDER MY SKIN

from BORN TO DANCE

Words and Music by
COLE PORTER

Bb7
Ebmaj7
3fr
Eb6
you're real - ly a part of me.
I've
Fm7
Fm7/Bb
Bb7
Ebmaj7
3fr
got you
un - der my skin.
Eb6
Fm7
Bb7
I tried so
not to give
Ebmaj7
3fr
Eb6
Fm7b5
in.
I said to my - self, "This af -
3
3
3
3

Fm7♭5/B♭
B♭7
D
E♭maj7
3 fr
E♭6
fair nev - er will go so well." But
Dm7
G7
Cdim7
C
why should I try to re - sist when, dar-ling, I know so well?
A♭m6
4 fr
A♭m6/B♭
6 fr
B♭7
E♭maj7
3 fr
I've got you under my skin.
E♭6
Fm7/E♭
B♭7/E♭
I'd sac - ri - fice an - y - thing, come what might, for the

Ebmaj7
3fr
Eb7
Fm7/Eb
sake of hav - ing you near, in spite of a warn - ing voice that
Fm7b5/Eb
6fr
Ebmaj7
3fr
Edim7
Bb7/F
Bb7
comes in the night and re - peats and re - peats in my ear: "Don't you
Cm
3fr
Ab
4fr
Bb7/Ab
2fr
Eb/G
3fr
F#dim7
know, lit-tle fool, you nev-er can win. Use your men -
Fm7
Bb7
Eb
3fr
tal - i - ty, wake up to re - al - i - ty."

A♭
4fr
A♭m6
4fr
But each time I do, just the thought of you makes me
E♭/G
3fr
B♭m/D♭
C7
Fm
stop be-fore I be - gin, 'cause I've got you
rit.
a tempo
B♭7♭9
E♭
3fr
1
E♭maj7
3fr
E♭6
2
Fm7
B♭7
under my skin. I've
poco rall.
E♭
3fr
B♭7
E♭
3fr
8va bassa

I'M GONNA LOCK MY HEART
(AND THROW AWAY THE KEY)

By JIMMY EATON
and TERRY SHAND

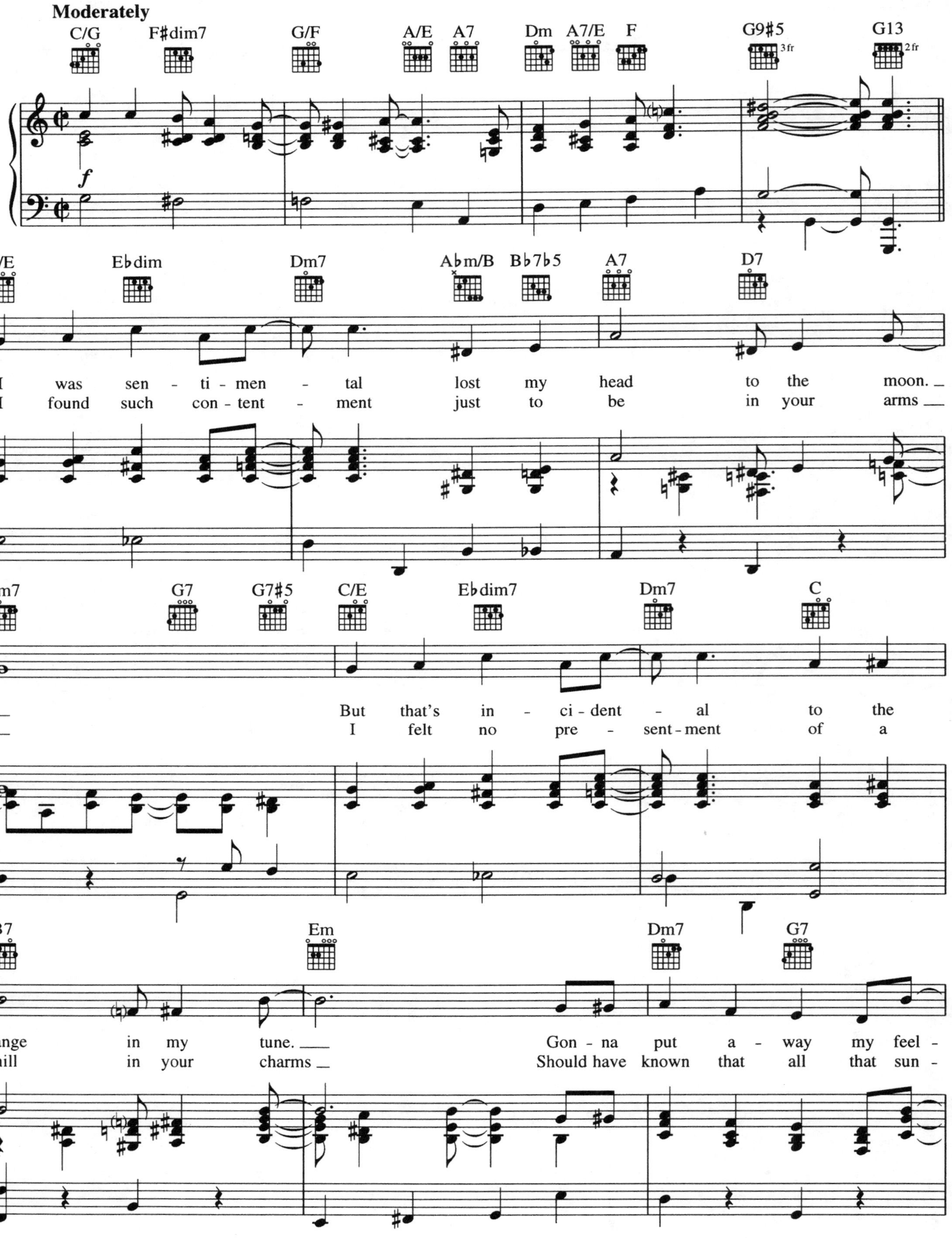
Moderately
C/G F♯dim7 G/F A/E A7 Dm A7/E F G9♯5 G13
3fr
2fr
f
C/E E♭dim Dm7 A♭m/B B♭7♭5 A7 D7
I was sen - ti - men - tal lost my head to the moon.
I found such con - tent - ment just to be in your arms
Dm7 G7 G7♯5 C/E E♭dim7 Dm7 C
But that's in - ci - dent - al to the
I felt no pre - sent - ment of a
B7 Em Dm7 G7
change in my tune. Gon - na put a - way my feel -
chill in your charms Should have known that all that sun -

C/E
E♭dim7
Dm
G7
C
- ings lay my love up - on the shelf. For the
- shine would be bound to turn to rain. But my
Em
C
B7
Em
Cm6/E♭
C/D
C♯
D
D7
on - ly way to keep it is to keep it to my -
fool - ish heart will nev - er get the best of me a -
CHORUS
G7
G7♯5
C6
G7♯5
self:
gain:
I'm gon - na lock my heart and
C
G7♯5
C
Cmaj7
C6
G7♯5
throw a - way the key. I'm

C
A7
Dm7
wise to all those tricks you've played on me.
G7
Dm7
G7
I'm gon - na turn my back on love gon - na
C
C/B
Am
D9
4fr
snub the moon a - bove seal all my win - dows up with tin
G7
Gdim7
G7
G7#5
C
G7#5
C
G7#5
so the love bug can't get in. I'm gon - na park my ro - mance right a - long the

C Cmaj7 C6 C7
curb hang a sign up - on my heart "Please don't dis - turb."
F A7/E Dm F6 F#dim7
And if I nev - er fall in love a - gain, that's
C/G E7 A7 Eb7 D7 Dm7/G G7
soon e - nough for me, I'm gon - na lock my heart and throw a - way the
1 C G7#5
key. I'm gon - na
2 C F6/A Fm/Ab Dm7/G C
key.

I'M PUTTING ALL MY EGGS IN ONE BASKET

from the Motion Picture FOLLOW THE FLEET

Words and Music by
IRVING BERLIN

G+/C
C6/G
E
C#m/B
Em#7
C#m/B
in the fire is worse than not hav - ing an - y.
D7/A
G#dim7
Am
D7
G7
G7♭5
G7
I've had my share and from now on
C
F/G
G7
C
Cmaj7
C9
I'm put - ting all my eggs in one
mf
F
Dm7♭5
C/G
G7
bask - et. I'm bet - ting ev - 'ry-thing I've got on you.

C
Am
Dm
G7
C
F/G
G7
I'm giv - ing all
my love to one ba - by.
Cmaj7
C9
F6
Dm7♭5
C/G
Lord help me if
my ba - by don't come through.
Dm/G
Bdim7
C/B♭
I've got a great
big a - mount saved up in my love ac - count, hon - ey, and
F
F/C
A♭
A♭/E♭
Adim7

E♭7/B♭
E♭7
E♭7/B♭
E♭7
G7/D
G7♭9
G9/D
G7♯5♭9
I've de - ci - ded love di - vi - ded in two won't do. So
C
F/G
G7
C
Cmaj7
C9
I'm put - ting all my eggs in one
F
Dm7♭5
C/G
G7
bask - et. I'm bet - ting ev - 'ry-thing I've got on you.
1
C
Am
Dm
G7
2
C
Dm7/G
C6

I'VE GOT MY LOVE TO KEEP ME WARM

from the 20th Century Fox Motion Picture ON THE AVENUE

Words and Music by
IRVING BERLIN

B♭9
E♭/G
B7/F♯
Fm7
B♭9
E♭6
G♭dim
I've got my love to keep me warm.
Fm7
B♭7
E♭/G
G♭dim
G♭m6
G♭dim
Fm
I can't re - mem - ber a worse De -
B♭7♭5
A♭/B♭
B♭9
Am7♭5
D7
D7♭9
cem - ber; just watch those i - ci - cles form.
F♯dim
Fm7
B♭7
B♭9sus
What do I care if i - ci - cles form?

B♭9
E♭/G
B7/F♯
Fm7
B♭9
E♭6
I've got my love to keep me warm.
D7♭9
Gm
D+
Off with my o - ver - coat,
Gm7
C7
Fm
G7
C7
off with my glove. I need no o - ver - coat,
Fm
Fm7♭5
B♭7
Fm7/C
B♭7/D
E♭/G
G♭dim
G♭m6
G♭dim
I'm burn-ing with love. My heart's on fire, the

Fm
B♭7♭5
A♭/B♭
B♭9
Am7♭5
D7
D7♭9
flame grows high - er. So I will weath - er the storm.
F♯dim
Fm7
B♭7
What do I care how much it may storm?
B♭9sus
B♭9
E♭/G
B7/F♯
Fm7
B♭9
I've got my love to keep me warm.
1
E♭
G♭dim7
Fm9
B♭7/D
The
2
E♭
D♭6/9
E♭6

IF YOU CAN'T SING IT
(YOU'LL HAVE TO SWING IT)
from the Paramount Picture RHYTHM ON THE RANGE

Words and Music by
SAM COSLOW

Am6
5 fr
B7
Em
A7
Dm
Dm/F
sor - ry it's all o - ver now." When from the gal - ler - y
Em
Em/G
Dm/F
Dm
G7
'way up high, there sud - den - ly came this mourn - ful cry:
C
C9
F
F9#11
"Mis - ter Pa - ga - ni - ni please play my rhap - so - dy and
C/E
Gm7
3 fr
A7#5
A7
D9
4 fr
if you can-not play it, won't you sing it, and if you can't sing it,

G+ G7♭9 C C♯m7♭5 G9 B7/D♯
you'll sim - ply have to swing it, I said swing it, I mean
C/E C C♯m7♭5 G9 G7♯5 C C9
swing it and dong ding it. Oh, Mis - ter Pa - ga - ni - ni, we
F F9 C/E Gm7
breath - less - ly a - wait your mas - ter - ful ba - ton, go on and
3 3
A7♯5 A7 D9 G+ G7♭9
sling it; And if you can't sling it you'll sim - ply have to

C
C#m7♭5
2fr
G9
B7/D#
C/E
C#m7♭5
2fr
swing it, I said swing it and scad-a-ma - fa and fad-a-ma-
G9
G7
E7
sca. We've heard your rep-er-toire, and at the fi-nal bar, we
Am
D7
greet - ed you with wild ap - plause, but what a great o-va - tion,
F
Dm
your in-ter-pre-ta - tion, of wo - ho - o - o - o would cause

C
C9
F
F9♯11
Mis - ter Pa - ga - ni - ni, now don't you be a mean - ie, what
C/E
Gm7
3fr
A7♯5
A7
D9
4fr
have you up your sleeve, come on and spring it, and if you don't spring it,
G+
3fr
E7♭9
C
Am
Dm7
Dm7/F
F♯m7♭5
4fr
that means you'll have to swing it."
1
C
Dm7
G7
G7♯5
2
C
Fmaj7
C6

IN THE MOOD

By JOE GARLAND

D7
G6
C6
E♭7 Am7/D G6
G
C
G
D7
G6
C6
E♭7Am7/D G6
Fine
G6
G6/B B♭dim7 Am7
Am7/D D7♭9
G6
G6/B B♭dim7 Am7

Am7/D D7♭9
G6
G6/B
B♭dim7 Am7
Am7/D
D7
Ddim7
D7
E♭7 D7
G6
G6/B B♭dim7Am7
Am7/D D7♭9
G6
G6/B B♭dim7 Am7
Am7/D D7♭9
G
G6/B
Bdim7 Am7
Am7/D
D7
Ddim7
1.
D7
E♭7 D7
G6
2.
D7
E♭7 D7
G6
N.C.
D7♯5
G
D.S. al Fine

IS YOU IS, OR IS YOU AIN'T
(MA' BABY)
from FOLLOW THE BOYS
from FIVE GUYS NAMED MOE

Words and Music by BILLY AUSTIN
and LOUIS JORDAN

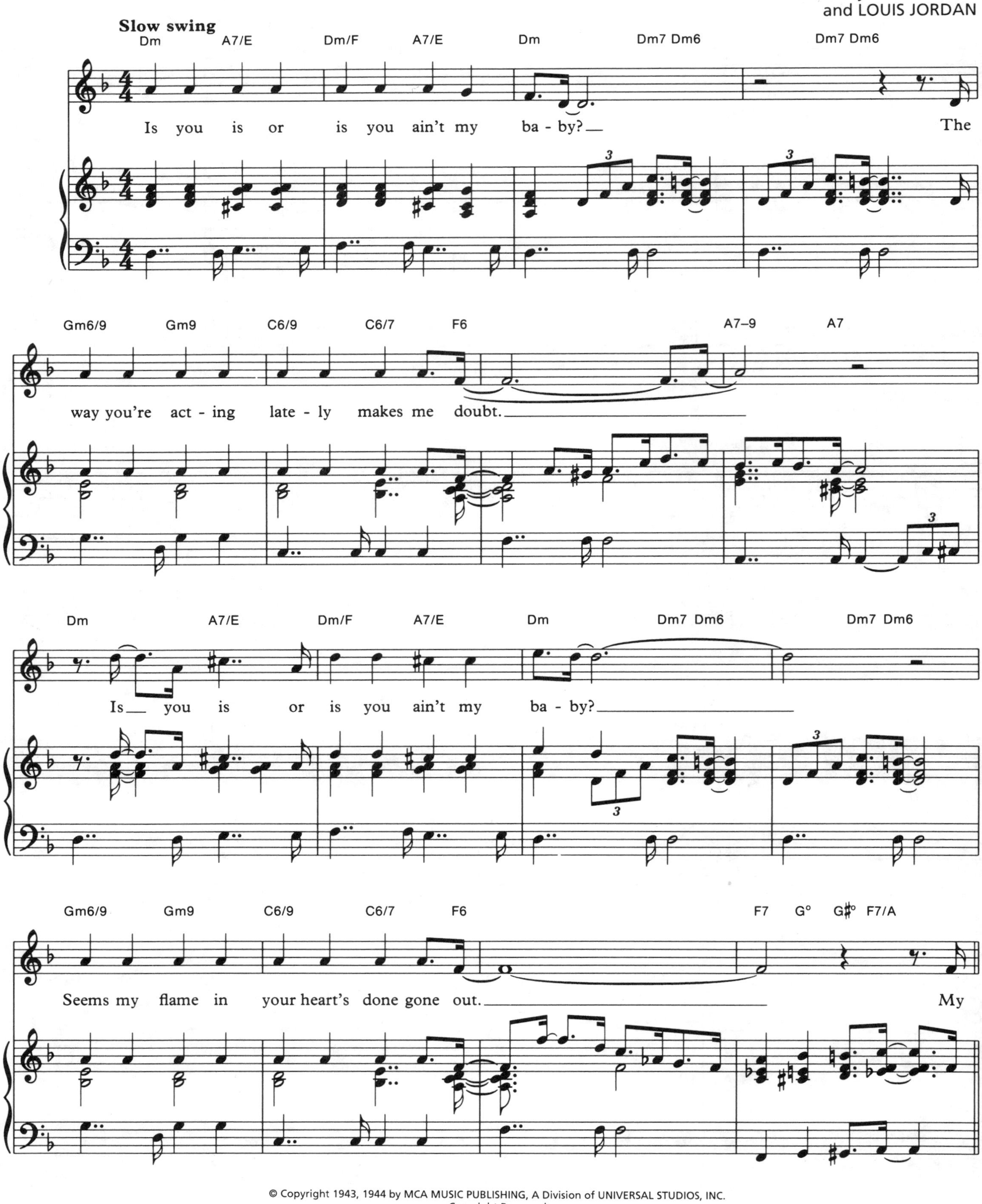
Slow swing
Dm A7/E Dm/F A7/E Dm Dm7 Dm6 Dm7 Dm6
Is you is or is you ain't my ba - by? The
Gm6/9 Gm9 C6/9 C6/7 F6 A7–9 A7
way you're act - ing late - ly makes me doubt.
Dm A7/E Dm/F A7/E Dm Dm7 Dm6 Dm7 Dm6
Is you is or is you ain't my ba - by?
Gm6/9 Gm9 C6/9 C6/7 F6 F7 G° G♯° F7/A
Seems my flame in your heart's done gone out. My

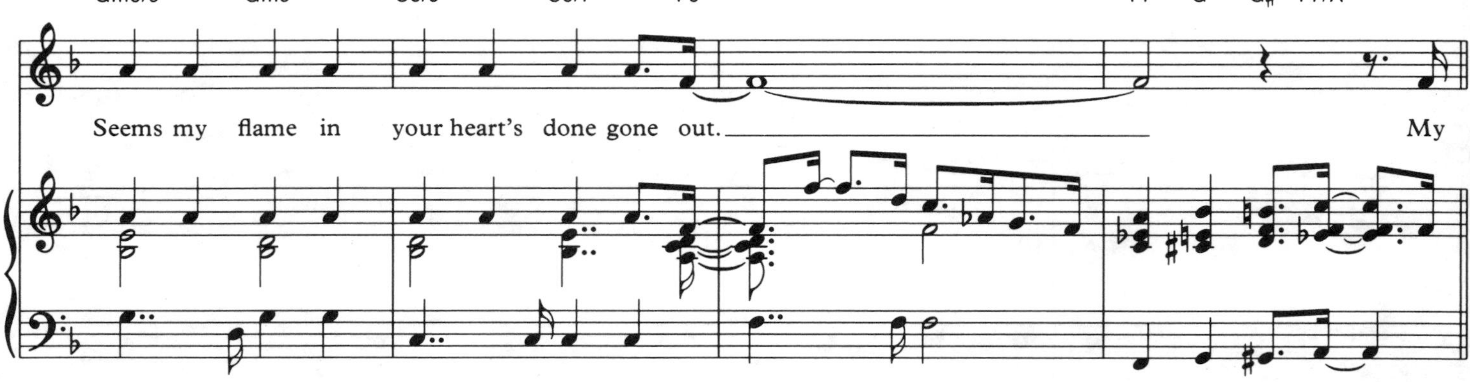

B♭6
B°
B♭6
F6
Gm7
F
friends say I could do a lot bet - ter, if this keeps up I'll soon need a nurse. I
Gm9
G9
Gm7
C
C♯
know I can't do a-ny bet-ter, but be - lieve me I could do a lot worse.
F♯m
C♯7/G♯
F♯m/A
C♯7/G♯
F♯m
F♯m7F♯m6
F♯m7F♯m6
Is you is or is you ain't my ba - by? The
B9
E6/7
A6
G♯m–5
C♯
way you're act - ing late - ly makes me doubt.

F♯m C♯7/G♯ F♯m/A C♯7/G♯ F♯m F♯m7 F♯m6 F♯m7 F♯m6
Is__ you is or is you ain't my ba - by?
B9 E6/7 A6 A7 Bm7 A7/C♯
Seems my flame in your heart's done gone out. When the
D6 Dm6 C♯m7–5
moon goes down in the dawn - ing__ and the sun comes up in the morn -
F♯ Bm9 E
- ing,__ don't let the sun catch you cry - in'. When the

C♯m7–5
F♯
Bm9
moon goes down in the dawn - ing, don't let the sun catch you cry - in' if your
E
F♯6
G°
E7/G♯
A6
G6
A6
G6
ba - by don't want you no more.
No more.
A6
G6
A6
G6
A6
G6
No more.
A6
G6
E♭13
D13
D♭13
C13
C♭13
B♭13
A13

IT COULD HAPPEN TO YOU

from the Paramount Picture AND THE ANGELS SING

Words by JOHNNY BURKE
Music by JAMES VAN HEUSEN

Bb7 Bb7/Ab Eb/G Bbm7/Ab Gm7b5
show your scorn; watch your - self, I
Ab Am7 D7sus D7 G
warn you. Hide your
G#dim7 Am A#dim7
heart from sight, lock your dreams at night.
G/B C B7 Bm7b5 E7
It could hap - pen to you.

Am7
Cm
3fr
G
F♯m7♭5
4fr
B7
Don't count stars or you might stum - ble,
Em
C7/E
A7
Am7
Am6
5fr
A♭9
4fr
Some - one drops a sigh, and down you tum - ble.
G
G♯dim7
Am
Keep an eye on Spring, run when
A♯dim7
G/B
C
church bells ring. It could hap - pen to
3

B7
Bm7♭5
E7
Am7
you.
All
I
Cm
3fr
G/D
Bm7♭5
E7
did
was
won - der
how
your
arms
would
be
Am7
D9
4fr
D7♭9
4fr
1
G
Em
and
it
hap - pened
to
me!
Am7
D7♯5(♭9)
4fr
2
G
C6
C9
G
me!

IT DON'T MEAN A THING
(IF IT AIN'T GOT THAT SWING)
from SOPHISTICATED LADIES

Words and Music by DUKE ELLINGTON
and IRVING MILLS

Gm
Gm/F
E♭7
D7
sweet?
It ain't the mel-o - dy,
Gm
Gm/F
Em7♭5
E♭7
Gm
Gm/F
Em7♭5
E♭7
it ain't the mu - sic,
there's some-thing else that makes the
A7/E
E♭7
D7
Gm
Gm/F
tune com - plete.
It don't mean a thing if it
E♭7
D7
Gm
C7/G
ain't got that swing,
(doo wah, doo wah,

Gb7b5
Cm7/F
Bb6
D7#5
doo wah, doo wah, doo wah, doo wah, doo wah, doo wah.) It
Gm
Gm/F
Em7b5
Eb7
D7#5
Db7
C7
don't mean a thing, all you got to do is sing,
C7/G
Gb7b5
Cm7/F
(doo wah, doo wah, doo wah, doo wah, doo wah, doo wah, doo wah, doo
Bb6
F#dim7
Bb7
Eb
wah.) It makes no diff-'rence if it's sweet or hot,

F♯dim7 C7 F♯dim7 C7 F7
just give that rhy - thm ev - 'ry - thing you got.
G7 D7♯5 Gm Gm/F E♭7 D7
Oh, it don't mean a thing if it ain't got that swing,
Gm C7/G G♭7♭5
(doo wah, doo wah, doo wah, doo wah, doo wah,
Cm7/F
doo wah, doo wah, doo wah.)
1 B♭6 D7♯5
It
2 B♭6
wah.)
3fr

IT'S ALL RIGHT WITH ME

from CAN-CAN

Words and Music by
COLE PORTER

F9
Cm
Fm
in the wrong style tho' your smile is love - ly, it's the wrong smile,
Bb
Bb9
Bb7
Bbm6
C9
F9
it's not {her / his} smile but such a love - ly smile that It's All Right
mf
sf
Fm7
Bb7
Eb
Eb9
Ebdim
With Me. You can't know how hap - py I am that we
dim.
mf
Abm/Eb
Fdim/Eb
Eb
Ebmaj7
Eb6
Bbm6
met, I'm strange - ly at - tract - ed to you, There's some - one I'm
C7-9
F7
Fm6
G7
Cm6
try - ing so hard to for - get. Don't you want to for - get some - one too?

G F G7 Cm F9
It's the wrong game with the wrong chips, tho' your
Cm Fm Bb Bb9
lips are tempt - ing, they're the wrong lips, They're not {her / his} lips,
Bb7 Bbm6 C9 F9 F7
but they're such tempt - ing lips that if some night you're
Bb9 Gm D Fm7 Bb7 Ebmaj7 Eb7 Eb7+5 Abmaj7 Ab7
free, dear, It's All Right, It's All Right With
F9 Fm7 1 Eb G7 2 Eb
Me. It's the
mp
sf
cresc.
dim.
f
Ped.
8va

JUKE BOX SATURDAY NIGHT

from STARS ON ICE

Words by AL STILLMAN
Music by PAUL McGRANE

F7
- ler help to make things bright,
B♭
F A♭dim7 Gm7 C9 F
4 fr
3 fr
mix - in' hot licks with va - nil - la, juke box Sat - ur - day night.
G♭6 F6 Cm7 F7 Cm7 F7
3fr
They put noth - in' past us,
B♭ F+ B♭ Dm7 G7
me and hon - ey lamb, mak - ing one coke

Dm7
G7
C7
Gm7
3fr
C7
last us
Till it's time to scram.
F
Mon - ey, we real - ly don't need that,
We make out all
F7
B♭
right,
let - tin' the oth - er guy feed that
F
A♭dim7
4fr
Gm7
3fr
C9
F
1
F6
Gm7
3fr
C9
2
F
G♭6
F6
juke box Sat - ur - day night.

IT'S DE-LOVELY

from RED, HOT AND BLUE!

Words and Music by
COLE PORTER

*Pronounced "delukes"

THE JOINT IS JUMPIN'

from AIN'T MISBEHAVIN'

Words by ANDY RAZAF and J.C. JOHNSON
Music by THOMAS "FATS" WALLER

F C7 F F#dim Gm7 C7 F7
ev - 'ry - thing is in full swing_ when you hear some - bod - y shout: (Here 'tis)
Bb Bdim Cm7 F7 Bb Bdim Cm7 F7
This joint is jump - in', it's real - ly jump - in'.
This joint is jump - in', it's real - ly jump - in'.
Bb Bb7 Eb Edim Bb F7 Bb
Come in cats_ an' check_ your hats,_ I mean_ this joint_ is jump - in'.
Ev - 'ry Mose_ is on ___ his toes,_ I mean_ the joint_ is jump - in'.
D A7 D A7 D A7 D C7
The pi - an - o's thump - in', the danc - ers bump - in'.
No time for talk - in', it's time_ for walk - in'. (Yes!)

F
C7
F
F#dim
C7
F7
This here spot_ is more than hot,_ in fact the joint is jump - in'.
Grab a jug_ and cut the rug,_ I mean this joint is jump - in'.
Bb7
Edim
Bb7
Eb
Bb7
Eb
Check your weap - ons at the door,_ be sure to pay your quar - ter.
Get your pig feet, beer and gin,_ there's plen - ty in the kitch - en.
C7
F9
C7+5
F7
Burn your leath - er on the floor,_ grab an - y - bod - y's daugh - ter.
Who is that that just came in?_ Just look at the way he's switch - in'.
Bb
Bdim
Cm7
F7
Bb
Bdim
Cm7
F7
The roof is rock - in', the neigh-bor's knock - in'.
Don't mind the hour,_ 'cause I'm in pow - er.

Bb Bb7 Eb Edim 1. Bb F7 Bb F7
We're all bums_ when the wag-on comes._ I mean_ this joint is jump - in'. Let it beat!
I got bail_ if we go to jail._ I mean_
2. Bb Eb Bb F+ Bb Bdim Cm7 F9 Bb Bdim
_ this joint is jump - in'. This joint is jump - in', It's real - ly jump-
Cm7 F7 Bb Bb7 Eb Ebm Bb Eb
in. We're all bums_ when the wag - on comes,_ I mean_ this joint is jump-
Bb F+ Bb Bb7 Eb Ebm Bb Bb+ Gm7 C7 F7 Bb
in'. Don't give your right name. No, No, No!

LAZYBONES

Words and Music by HOAGY CARMICHAEL
and JOHNNY MERCER

F7
A♭7
4fr
G7
Long as there's a wa - ter - mel - on on the vine,
A♭7
4fr
G7
C
F
C
A7
ev' - ry - thing is fine. You got no time to work, you got no
D7
time to play, bus - y do - in' noth - in' all the
G7
G7♯5
C
F7
A♭7
4fr
G7
live - long day. You won't ev - er change no mat - ter what I say,

Ab7
G7
C
F
C
C
F
4fr
you're just made that way.
La - zy - bones,
C
F
C
F
G7#5
C
C7
sleep - in' in the sun,
how you 'spec' to get your day's work done?
Abdim
Gdim
D7
Gm
Dm
Ab7
G7
F
3fr
Nev - er get your day's work done,
sleep - in' in the noon - day
C
G7
C
F
C
F
sun.
La - zy - bones,
sleep - in' in the shade,
3
3

C
F
G7#5
C
C7
A♭dim
Gdim
D7
Gm
4fr
3fr
how you 'spec' to get your corn meal made? Nev - er get your corn meal
Dm
A♭7
4fr
G7
F
C
F
C
made sleep - in' in the eve - nin' shade. When
F
F6
Fmaj7
F6
C
G7
'ta - ters need spray - in, I bet you keep pray - in' the bugs fall off of the
C
F7
E♭7
D7
G7
vine. And when you go fish - in' I bet you keep wish - in' the

D7
Dm7/G
G7
C
F
fish won't grab at your line.
La - zy - bones,
C
F
C
F
G7♯5
C
C7
loaf - in' thru the day,
how you 'spec' to make a dime that way?
Bdim
B♭dim7
D7
Gm
3fr
Dm
A♭7
4fr
G7
F
Nev - er make a dime that way well look - y here, He nev - er heared a word I
1
C
G7
2
C
say!
say!
R.H.

LAZY RIVER

Words and Music by HOAGY CARMICHAEL
and SIDNEY ARODIN

D7
D♭7
C7
F♯dim
Up a la - zy riv - er by the old mill - run, that
G7
G6
A♭9
G9
la - zy, la - zy riv - er in the noon - day sun,
C7
C6
D♭7
C7
lin - ger in the shade of a kind old tree;
F
C7/G
A♭dim
F
F7
E7
E♭7
Throw a - way your trou - bles, dream a dream with me.

D7
Db7
4fr
C7
F#dim
Up a la - zy riv - er where the rob - in's song a -
G7
G6
Ab9
G9
Bb
Bdim
wakes a bright new morn - ing, we can loaf a - long. Blue skies up a-bove,
F/C
E7
Eb6
G9
C7
F
ev - 'ry one's in love, up a la - zy riv - er, how hap - py you can be,
1
2
F7
Eb7
F6
E6
up a la - zy riv - er with me. me.

LEAP FROG

Music by
JOE GARLAND

C
1
2
leap frog. Each day a
leap frog.
You just
A♭9
G9
leap and look for brand new charms. If you must jump, jump in my arms. You hold
C6
Dm7
me tight then hop from sight and that
G7
G7+5
D.S. al Coda
ain't right. You say you
CODA
C
C9♯11
leap frog.

LET'S DANCE

Words by FANNY BALDRIDGE
Music by GREGORY STONE and JOSEPH BONINE

Dm7
G7
G7+5
we go where sweet mu - sic weaves her spell o - ver us.
C6
Cdim
C6
Your cheek kiss - ing
F6
Bb7
F6
D9
mine, my sweet, thrills me through, dear.
C6
Em7
Gm6
A+
A7
Ah, sweet mel - o - dy, come guide our
D9
G9
G7-9
C6
feet. Let's Dance !
8va

LOVE IS JUST AROUND THE CORNER

from the Paramount Picture HERE IS MY HEART

Words and Music by LEO ROBIN
and LEWIS E. GENSLER

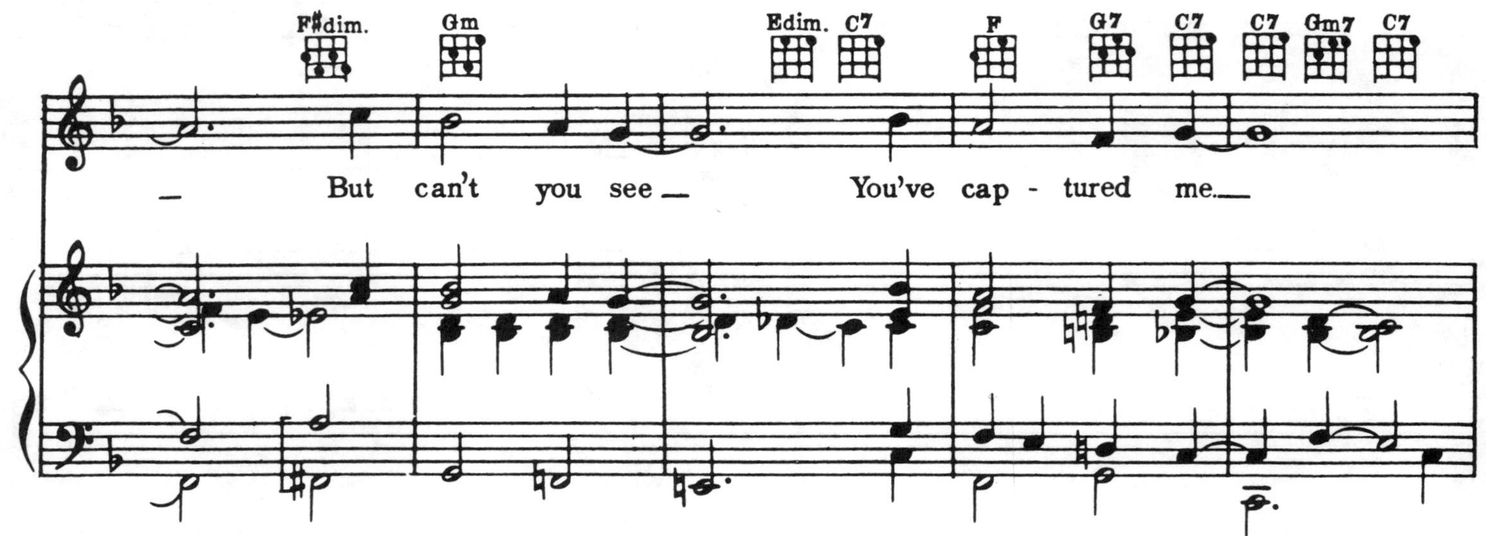

F
C7
F
C7
F
C7
F
Be - ing so glam - or - ous Can't you be am - or - ous just with me?
F
F#dim.
Ab7
C
F#dim.
G9
G9-5
C7
Bb
Am
E
Make it soon, Take a look at the moon-oo - - - -
Refrain
G7
C7
F
G7
C7
F
mp-mf
Love is just a round the cor-ner, An - y co - zy lit - tle cor-ner,
mp-mf
G7
C7
F
Cm
D7
G9
C7
F
Love is just a-round the cor - ner when I'm a-round you.

G7 C7 F G7 C7
I'm a sen - ti - men - tal mourn - er, And I could - n't be for -
F G7 C7 F Cm D7 G9 C7
lorn - er When you keep me on a - cor - ner just wait - ing for
F A7 Dm A7
you Ve - nus de Mi - lo was not - ed for her
Dm G7 C#dim. G7 C#dim.
charms, But strict - ly be - tween us, You're cut - er than Ve - nus and

G7
G♯dim.
G9
G7
C7
G7
C7
what's more you got arms.
8va
So let's go cud - dle in a
F
G7
C7
F
cor - ner
An - y co - zy lit - tle cor - ner
G7
C7
F
Cm
D7
G9
C7
1 F
G9
C7
Love is just a-round the cor - ner and I'm a-round you
2 F
F
E
E♭
D
C♯
D
E♭
E
F
you O-o-o
pp

LOVELY TO LOOK AT
from ROBERTA

Words by DOROTHY FIELDS and JIMMY McHUGH
Music by JEROME KERN

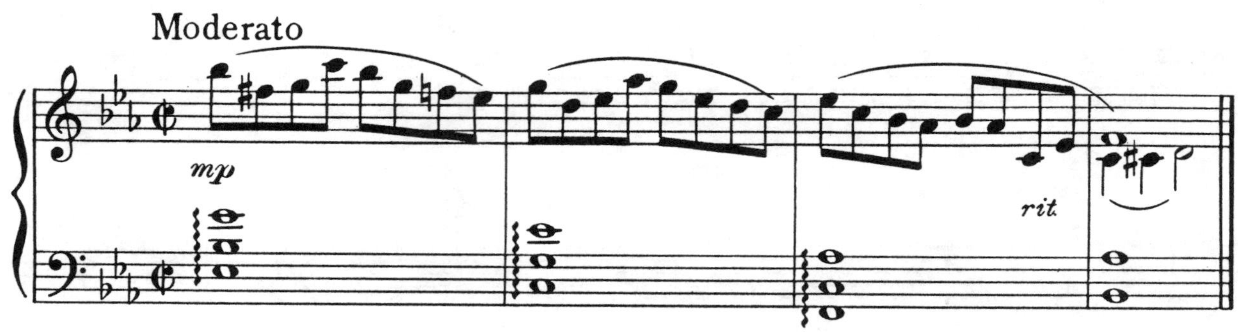

Gb
Gb6
Gb
Ab7
gown can al - most speak, If it is
wear, But just an air, Of great re -
Bb7
(Guitar tacet)
chic. Should you se - lect the right ef - fect, you can - not
pose. You are quite per - fect from your head down to your
quasi cadenza
Bb7
Bb9
miss, You may be sure,
toes Both night and day,
Fm7
Bb7
He will tell you this.
I am moved to say.
rall.

Refrain (gracefully)
Eb
Eb(F)
Eb(Ab)
Ebdim
Love - ly to look at, De - light - ful to know and
mf
Bb7
Bb9
Bb7
heav - en to kiss. A com - bin -
Bb9
Bb7
a - tion like this, Is quite my
Eb6
Edim
Fm7
Bb9
3
most im - pos - si - ble scheme come true, Im - a - gine find - ing a dream like you! You're

Eb
Eb(F)
Eb(Ab)
Cm6
love - ly to look at, It's thrill - ing to hold you
D7
G7
C9
F7
ter - ri - bly tight.
For
Bb7
Ab6
we're to - geth - er, the moon is new, And oh, it's love - ly to look at you to -
Eb
Fm
Bb7
B9
night!
You're
p

MAKIN' WHOOPEE!

from WHOOPEE!

E7
A
A7
Wed-dings make a lot of peo-ple sad. But if you're not the groom, they're not so
D7
G
D7
bad. An-oth-er bride an-oth-er June, an-oth-er
year or may-be less, what's this I
pf
G
G7
C
Am
Am7♭5
G/D
sun - ny hon-ey moon. An-oth-er sea-son, an-oth-er
hear? Well, can't you guess? She feels neg-lect-ed, and he's sus-
E♭
E♭7
D7
G
Am7/E♭
D7
rea-son for mak-in' whoop-ee! A lot of
pect-ed of mak-in' whoop-ee! She sits a-

G
D7
G
G7
shoes a lot of rice, the groom is nerv - ous he an-swers
lone 'most ev - 'ry night he does - n't 'phone her he does - n't
C
Am
Am7♭5
G
E♭
E♭7
D7
twice. It's real - ly kill - ing that he's so will - ing to make
write. He says he's "bu - sy" but she says "is he?" he's mak-in'
G
A♭dim7
Am
whoop-ee! Pic - ture a lit - tle love-nest,
whoop-ee! He does - n't make much mon - ey,
Cm
G
A♭dim7
down where the ros - es cling. Pic - ture the same sweet
on - ly five thou - sand per. Some judge who thinks he's

Am
Cm
G
love - nest, think what a year can bring. He's wash - ing
fun - ny, says "you'll pay six to her." He says, "now
D7
G
G7
dish - es and ba - by clothes he's so am - bi - tious he e - ven
judge, sup-pose I fail?" The judge says "budge right in - to
C
Am
Am7♭5
G/D
E♭
E♭7
D7
sews. But don't for - get, folks that's what you get, folks, for mak - in'
jail. You'd bet - ter keep her, I think it's cheap - er, than mak - in'
1
G
G/F
F/E♭
E/D
E♭/D♭
D/C
2
G
D+
G
whoop-ee! An - oth - er whoop-ee!"

MANHATTAN

from the Broadway Musical THE GARRICK GAIETIES

Words by LORENZ HART
Music by RICHARD RODGERS

Moderately

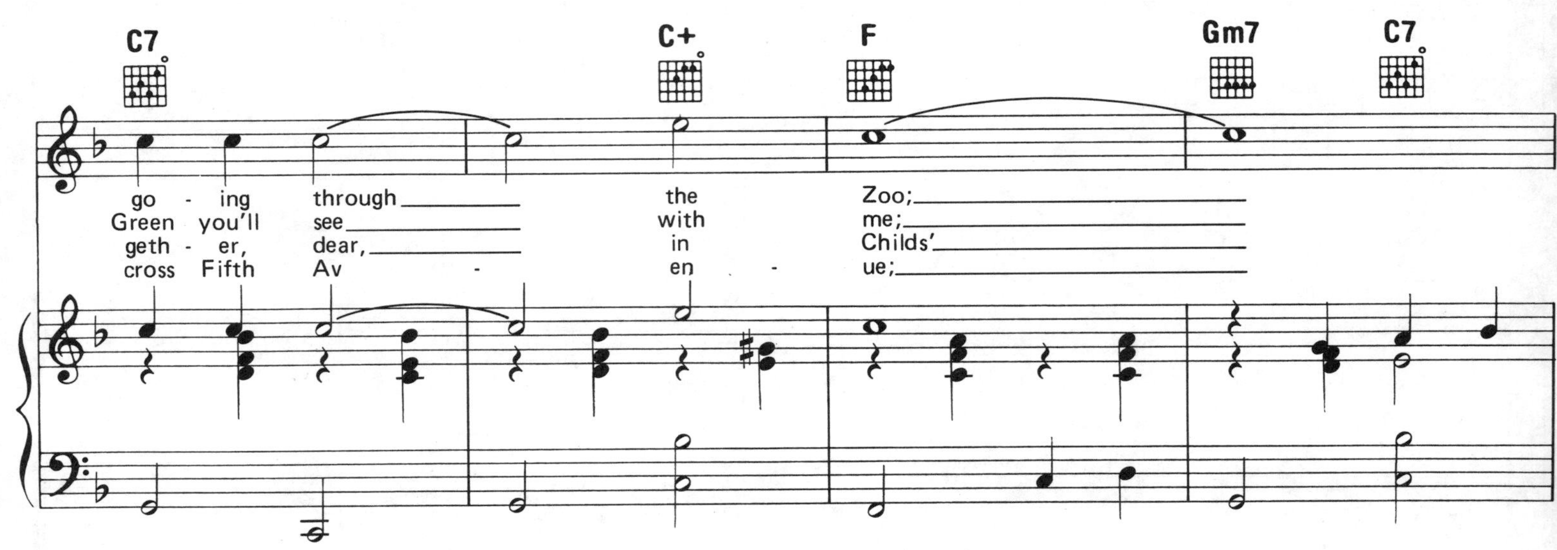

F A♭dim Gm C7 C♯dim Dm7 Am A♭dim
It's ver - y fan - cy On old De - lan - cey Street, you know; The sub - way
We'll bathe at Bright - on The fist you'll fright - en When you're in; Your bath - ing
We'll go to Cone - y And eat bo - log - ny on a roll; In Cen - tral
As black as on - yx We'll find the Bron - nix Park Ex - press; Our Flat - bush
G7 Gm7 C7 Gm C7 F D7
charms us so, When balm - y breez - es blow to and fro; And tell me what street
suit so thin Will make the shell - fish grin Fin to fin; I'd like to take a
Park, we'll stroll Where our first kiss we stole, Soul to soul; And for some high fare
flat, I guess Will be a great suc - cess. More or less; A short va - ca - tion
Gm C7 F A♭dim Gm7 C7 Gm7 C7
com - pares with Mott Street in Ju - ly, Sweet push carts gent - ly glid - ing
sail on Ja - mai - ca Bay with you; And fair Can - ar - sies Lakes we'll
We'll go to "My Fair La - dy", say, We'll hope to see it close some
On In - spir - a - tion Point we'll spend And in the sta - tion house we'll

Am7-5
D7
Gm7
B♭m
by:
view
day
end
The great big cit - y's a wond - 'rous toy Just
The cit - y's bus - tle can - not des - troy The
The cit - y's clam or can nev - er spoil The
But Civ - ic Vir - tue can not des - troy The
F/C
G7
F
A♭dim
G7
C7
made for a girl and boy We'll turn Man - hat - tan In - to an isle of
dreams of a girl and boy We'll turn Man - hat - tan In - to an isle of
dreams of a boy and goil We'll turn Man - hat - tan In - to an isle of
dreams of a girl and boy We'll turn Man - hat - tan In - to an isle of
1,2,3
F
A♭dim
Gm7
C7
4
F
B♭/C
C7
F
joy.
joy.
joy.
joy.

MY IDEAL

from the Paramount Picture PLAYBOY OF PARIS

Words by LEO ROBIN
Music by RICHARD A. WHITING and NEWELL CHASE

Cmi.
D7
Gmi.
Can't be or - dered a la carte I won - der if she he will
C7
Bb
Cmi.7
F7
Fmi.7
Bb+
be Al-ways a fan - ta - sy.
rall.
REFRAIN
p-mf
Eb
C9
Fmi.
Db7
C7
Will I ev - er find the girl boy in my mind The one who is My I -
p-mf a tempo
F7
Bb7
Fmi.
Bb7
G7
deal. May - be she's he's a dream and yet she he might be.

Cmi.
F7
B7
Bb7
Eb
C9
Just a-round the cor-ner wait-ing for me Will I rec-og-nize a
Fmi.
Db7
C7
F7
light in {her his} eyes That no oth-er eyes re-veal.
Or
Al-
Fmi.
Abmi.
Eb
Cdim.
Eb
Cmi.
Fmi.
Bb7
will I pass {him her} by and nev-er e-ven know that {he she} is My I-
tho' {she he} may be late I trust in fate and so I wait for My I-
1.
2.
Eb
Cdim.
Fmi.
Bb7
Eb
Cmi.
Eb7
Fmi.
Bb7
Eb
deal. deal. My I-deal.
Slow

MARIE

from the Motion Picture THE AWAKENING

Words and Music by
IRVING BERLIN

Am7♭5
D7
Cdim
Gm
find ro - mance is a game of chance, that is
G9
C7
C7♯5
F9
G♭9
F9
not all it seems to be. Ma -
B♭6
F♯9
rie, the dawn is break - ing. Ma -
F6
rie, you'll soon be wak -

D♭9
C9
ing, to find your heart is
Gm7
C7
F
C7
ach - ing. And tears will fall as
F
F7♯5
F7
B♭
you re - call the moon in all its
G♭9
F
splen - dor, the kiss so ver - y

D♭9
C9
ten - der. The words
will you sur - ren - der, to
Gm7
C7
F
C9
1 F
me Ma - rie.
G♭9
F9
2 F
E♭
E
F
Ma - rie.

MOOD INDIGO

from SOPHISTICATED LADIES

Words and Music by DUKE ELLINGTON,
IRVING MILLS and ALBANY BIGARD

Ab7
Abdim7
Gdim/Ab
Ab7
Cb7/Ab
Ab7
That feel - ing goes steal - in'
Db6
Gb7
Eb7#5
down to my shoes, while
Ab
Bb9
To Coda
Ebm
Eb7#5
I sit and sigh: "Go 'long,
Abmaj7
Ab6
Ab+
Ab
Ab
Abdim7
Ab
blues." Al - ways get that

B♭7
E♭9
D♭/E♭
E♭7
A♭/C
B♭dim7
B♭m7
E♭7
mood in - di - go, since my ba - by said good - bye.
A♭
A♭dim7
A♭
B♭7
4fr
In the eve - nin' when lights are low,
B♭9/F
E7♯5
E7
E♭7
D♭/F
D♭m/F♭
E♭7
I'm so lone - some I could cry.
A♭7
'Cause there's no - bod - y who cares a - bout me,

Db7
4fr
E7/D
Eb7
I'm just a soul who's blu - er than blue can be.
Ab
Abdim7
Ab
Bb7
When I get that mood in - di - go,
Eb9
Db/Eb
Eb7
1
Ab
Bbm7
Eb7
I could lay me down and die.
2
Ab
Bbm7
E7
Eb7
D.S. al Coda
die.
CODA
Ebm
Eb7#5
Ab6
3fr
Ab+
Ab
"Go 'long blues."
rit.

MOONGLOW

Words and Music by WILL HUDSON,
EDDIE DE LANGE and IRVING MILLS

Am7
Cm
3fr
G6/B
It must have been Moon - glow, 'way up in the
A9
Am7
Am7♭5
D9
4fr
blue. It must have been Moon - glow
G
E♭7/G
Am7/G
E♭7/G
G
Am7
that led me straight to you.
I still hear you
Cm
3fr
G6/B
A9
say - ing, "Dear one, hold me fast."

Am7
Am7♭5
D9
4fr
G
E♭7/G
And I start in pray - ing,
Oh Lord, please
Am7/G
E♭7/G
G
G9
F♯9
3fr
F9
let this last.
We
seemed to float right through the
E9
A9
air.
Heav-en - ly songs
D9
4fr
E♭9
D9
4fr
seemed to come from ev - 'ry - where.

Am7
Cm
3 fr
G6/B
And now when there's Moon - glow 'way up in the
A9
Am7
Am7♭5
D9
4 fr
blue, I al - ways re - mem - ber
1
G
E♭7/G
Am7/G
E♭7/G
G
D7
that Moon - glow gave me you.
2
G
E♭7/G
that Moon - glow
Am7/G
Am7♭5/G
4 fr
G
C
Cm
3 fr
Gmaj7
gave me you.

MY BABY JUST CARES FOR ME

Lyrics by GUS KAHN
Music by WALTER DONALDSON

A7
D7
G
A7
D7
G
some-one loves _ me too. _
Guess it's hard for
C7
G
C7
you to see _ just what an - y - one _ can see in me _ but it
A7
D7
sim - ply goes to prove what love _ can do. _
3
G
My ba - by don't care for shows, My ba - by don't
My ba - by's no Gil - bert fan, Ron Col - man is

Gmaj7/B
B♭dim7
Am
care for clothes, my ba - by just cares for me!
not her man, my ba - by just cares for me!
B7
Em
My ba - by don't care for furs and
My ba - by don't care for Law - rence
A7
D7
la - ces, my ba - by don't care for high - toned
Tib - bets, she'd rath - er have me a - round to
G
plac - es. My ba - by don't care for rings, or oth - er ex -
kib - bitz. Bud Rog - ers is not her style, and e - ven Che -

E7♭9
E7
pen - sive things, she's sen - si - ble as can
val - iers smile, is some-thing that she can't
Am
F♯7
be.
see.
My ba - by don't care who
I won-der what's wrong with
Bm
E7
Am
A7
D7
knows it, my ba - by just cares for
ba - by? My ba - by just cares for
1
G
Gdim7
D7
D+
me!
2
G
D7
G
me!
3

ON THE SUNNY SIDE OF THE STREET

Lyric by DOROTHY FIELDS
Music by JIMMY McHUGH

B♭
B♭dim
B♭9
C
Am7
with the sun in my heart.
All my wor - ry blew a -
D9
C
D9
G7
Dm7
G7
way
When you taught me how to say:
Grab your
rit.
C
G7
C
E7
Am6
C7
E
F
Fm
coat, and get your hat,
leave your wor - ry on the
mp
G7
Am
E7
Am
Cm
D7
door - step.
Just di - rect your feet
to the

Dm7 G7 C G7 C G7 C
sun - ny side of the street. Can't you hear a pit - ter
E7 Am6 C7 E F Fm G7 Am E7 Am Cm
pat? And that hap - py tune is your step. Life can be so
D7 Dm7 G7 C Fm6 Cdim
sweet, on the sun - ny side of the street. I used to
C7 Gm7 C7 Cdim C7 F6
walk in the shade with those blues on par - ade,

Gm7
Fdim
F
D7
Am7
D7
but I'm not a - fraid, this
G7
Gdim
G7
C
G7
C
Ro - ver crossed o - ver. If I nev - er have a
E7
Am6
C7
E
F
Fm
G7
Am
E7
Am
Cm
cent, I'll be rich as Rock - e - fel - ler. Gold dust at my
D7
Dm7
G7
C
feet, on the sun - ny side of the street.

OPUS ONE

Words and Music by
SY OLIVER

C7
peat an' re - peat, But if you can swing, it's got a good beat, And
A7
Am7
D9
G
C7
that's the main thing, to make with the feet, 'Cause ev - 'ry - one is swing - in' to - day,
G
Bb
Gm7
Cm7
Adim
So, I'll call it O - pus One! It's not for Sam - my Kaye,
Bb
G7+5
C9
F9+5
Db
Bbm7
Hey! hey! hey! it's O - pus One! It's

Ebm7
Cdim
Db
Db7
D7
got to swing, not sway.
May - be,
if
G
C7
Mis - ter Les Brown could make it re - nown
And Ray An - tho - ny could
A7
Am7
D9
swing it for me,
There's nev - er a doubt you'll knock your - self out,
When -
G
C7
1 G
G#dim
Am7
D7
2 G
Eb9
G6
ev - er you can hear O - pus One.
I'm

SATIN DOLL
from SOPHISTICATED LADIES

Words by JOHNNY MERCER and BILLY STRAYHORN
Music by DUKE ELLINGTON

Dm7 G7 Dm7 G7 Em7 A7
Ba - by shall we go out skip - pin' care - ful a - mi - go,
Em7 A7 Cm/Eb D7 Abm7 Db7-9
you're flip - pin' Speaks Lat - in that sat - in doll.
C6
Guitar Tacet
Gm7 C7 Gm7 C7
She's no - bod - y's fool, so I'm play - ing it cool as can be,
Fmaj7 Gbmaj7 Gmaj7 Abmaj7 Am7 D7
I'll give it a whirl, but I

Am7 D7 G7 Dm7 G7-9

ain't for no girl___ catch - ing me.___ *Spoken: Swich - E - Roo - ney*

Dm7 G7 Dm7 G7 Em7 A7

Tel - e - phone num - bers well you know, do - ing my rhum - bas

Em7 A7 Cm/Eb D7 Abm7 Db7-9

with u - no, And that 'n' my sat - in doll.___

1 C6 Guitar Tacet

2 C6

RAG MOP

Words and Music by JOHNNIE LEE WILLS
and DEACON ANDERSON

Chorus—After 2nd and 5th Verses
F6
Bb7
Rag Mop!
Rag Mop!
Rag Mop!
F6
C7
Rag Mop!
Rag Mop!
F6
Bb
C11
F6
1,2,3 4
C7
D.S. and Repeat
R - A - G - G, M - O - P - P, Rag Mop!
5
F6
F
F7
Bb
Bbm
F
C11
F6
Mop! Mop!

ROUTE 66

By BOBBY TROUP

F
F13
E♭13
C13
F6
B♭9
It winds from Chi - ca - go to L. A.,
mf
more than two thou-sand miles all the way.
f
Gm7
Get your kicks on Route Six - ty Six!
F/C
Now you go thru Saint Loo-ey Jop - lin, Mis-sour-i and

F/C
F7
B♭9
Ok - la - hom - a Cit - y is might - y pret - ty. You'll see Am - ar -
mf
F6/9
F
Bdim
F
Gm7
C7
il - lo, Gal - lup, New Mex - i - co; Flag-staff, Ar - i - zon - a;
f
Gm7
C7
F6/C
Cdim7
Gm7/C
C7
don't for - get Wi - no - na, King - man, Bar - stow, San Ber - nar - din - o. Won't
mp
cresc.
f
mf
F6
B♭9
F6
you get hip to this time - ly tip:
f

B♭9
When you make that Cal - i - for - nia trip.
mf
F6
Gm7
C13
Get your kicks on Route Six - ty Six!
f
mf
F
D7
C♯7
C7
no chord
F
B♭6
Bdim7
F/C
no chord
If you
Get your
mf
f
Gm7
C13
F
E13
F13
kicks on Route Six - ty Six!
dim.
p
f

SATURDAY NIGHT IS THE LONELIEST NIGHT OF THE WEEK

Words by SAMMY CAHN
Music by JULE STYNE

Refrain
B♭7
E♭
B♭7/F
E♭/G
Sat - ur - day night is the lone -
mf-f
B♭7/F
E♭
Gm7♭5
li - est night in the week,
C7♭9
Fm
D♭7/F
Dm7♭5
'Cause that's the night that my sweet - ie and I
D♭7/F
Fm
Fm7♭5
B♭7
used to dance cheek to cheek.

E♭
G7/D
Cm
I don't mind Sun - day night at all 'cause that's the
Am7♭5
D7♭9
Gm
G♭dim7
night friends come to call And
B♭/F
Gm7
Cm9
F9
Mon - day to Fri - day go fast and an -
B♭7
Fm7
B♭7
oth - er week is past, But

E♭
B♭7/F
E♭/G
B♭7/F
E♭
Sat - ur-day night is the lone - li-est night in the week,
mf
E♭
Gm7♭5
C7♭9
I sing the
Fm
D♭7/F
Fm6
D♭7/F
Fm
song that I sang for the mem - 'ries I u - sual-ly seek.
Fm7♭5
B♭7
E♭
G7/D
Un - til I hear you at the door

Cm
Am7♭5
Fm7/A♭
G7
Cm
Fm7♭5/A♭
Un - til you're in my arms once more
E♭/B♭
C7
Fm9
A♭maj7/B♭
Sat - ur - day night is the lone - li - est night in the week,
1
E♭
Fm7
E♭/G
Fm7/A♭
B♭+
2
E♭
Fm7
E♭
B♭13♭9
E♭

SHOO FLY PIE AND APPLE PAN DOWDY

Lyric by SAMMY GALLOP
Music by GUY WOOD

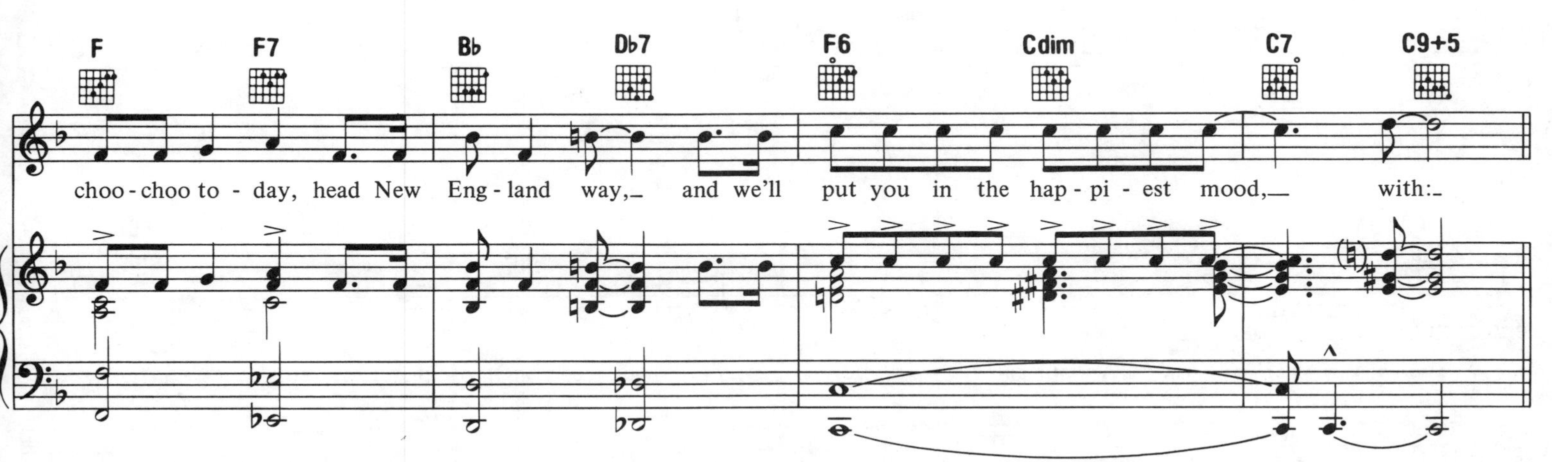

F
B♭
C7
F
Bdim
C7
Shoo-Fly Pie And Ap-ple Pan Dow-dy makes your eyes light up, Your tum-my say "how-dy,"
mp-mf
sf
F
B♭
F
B♭
F
F6
Shoo-Fly Pie And Ap-ple Pan Dow-dy, I nev-er get e-nough of that won-der-ful stuff.
F
B♭
C7
F
Bdim
C7
Shoo-Fly Pie And Ap-ple Pan Dow-dy makes the sun come out when Heav-ens are cloud-y,
sf
F
B♭
F
B♭
F
F6
Shoo-Fly Pie And Ap-ple Pan Dow-dy, I nev-er get e-nough of that won-der-ful stuff!

A7
D9
G7
Ma-ma! when you bake, Ma-ma! I don't want cake; Ma-ma!
f
C7
Cdim
Gm7
C7
F
for my sake go to the o-ven and make some ev-er-lov-in' sh, Shoo-Fly Pie And
ff
p
Bb
C7
F
Bdim
C7
F
Ap-ple Pan Dow-dy makes your eyes light up, Your 'tum-my' say "how-dy," Shoo Fly Pie And
sf
Bb
F
Bb
F
F6
F
F6
Ap-ple Pan Dow-dy I nev-er get e-nough of that won-der-ful stuff! won-der-ful stuff!

SHE'S FUNNY THAT WAY

Words by RICHARD A. WHITING
Music by NEIL MORET

C7♭5 B♭ Cm7 F7♭9 B♭7 B♭7♯5
I just have to stop and think, Why she fell for me. I'm
Can't help feel - ing it's a dream, Too good to be true.
rit.
mp
E♭ B♭7♯5 E♭ B♭7♯5 E♭ B♭7♯5
not much to look at; noth - in' to see, Just glad I'm liv - in' and
nev - er had noth - in', no one to care, That's why I seem to have
B♭m6 C7♯5 C7 A♭ A♭m
luck - y to be, I got a wom - an, cra - zy for me,
more than my share, I got a wom - an, cra - zy for me,
E♭ F9 Fm7 B♭7 B♭7♯5 E♭ B♭7♯5
She's fun - ny that way. I can't save a dol - lar,
She's fun - ny that way. When I hurt her feel - ings,

Eb
Bb7#5
Bbm6
C7#5
C7
ain't worth a cent, She does-n't hol - ler she'd live in a tent,
once in a while, Her on-ly an - swer is one lit-tle smile,
Ab
Abm
Fm
Bb7
I got a wom - an, cra-zy for me, She's fun-ny that
I got a wom - an, cra-zy for me, She's fun-ny that
way. Tho' she loves to work and slave for me ev-'ry
way. I can see no oth - er way and no bet-ter
Cm
day, She'd be so much bet - ter off if
plan, End it all and let her go to

Cm7
F7
B♭
Fm7
B♭7
B♭7♯5
E♭
B♭7♯5
I went a - way; But why should I leave her,
some bet - ter man; But I'm on - ly hu - man,
mp
E♭
B♭7♯5
E♭
B♭7♯5
B♭m6
C7♯5
C7
why should I go, She'd be un - hap - py with - out me I know,
cow - ard at best, I'm more than cer - tain she'd fol - low me west,
A♭
A♭m
1 E♭
Fm
B♭7
I got a wom - an, cra - zy for me, She's fun - ny that
I got a wom - an, cra - zy for me,
E♭
B♭7♯5
2 E♭
Cm
A♭
B♭9
E♭
way. I She's fun - ny that way.
rall.
p

SOMEBODY ELSE IS TAKING MY PLACE

Words and Music by DICK HOWARD,
BOB ELLSWORTH and RUSS MORGAN

Bb
G7
C7
face
Lit - tle you care for vows that you made
F7
Fdim
F7
Bb
Bb7
Eb
Lit - tle you care how much I have paid
My heart is
Bb
Bb7
G7
C7
F7
Eb
F7
ach - ing My heart is break - ing For some - bo - dy's tak - ing my
Bb
Bbdim
Cm7
F7
place.
Bb
Eb6
Ebm6
Bb
place.
rall.

SOMETIMES I'M HAPPY

Words by CLIFFORD GREY and IRVING CAESAR
Music by VINCENT YOUMANS

C7
F
heart,
beams
when
now
there will
you
be
C7
C+
F
are
in
not
the
near.
skies.
F7
B♭6
Adim
She: All
He: Tell
that
me
you
that
claim
you
must
will
be
be
B♭6
B♭m6
G7
true
true!
for
She: That
I'm
will
just
all
the
de - pend
same
as
on
you.
you

C7
dear!
rit.
Slowly
F
C7
F
Some - times I'm hap - py,
Some - times I'm
C7
F
C7
blue,
My dis - po - si - tion
F
C7
F
de - pends on you,
I nev - er

Am7♭5
Adim7
B♭
B♭dim7
B♭
B♭m6
mind the rain from the skies,
F/C
F
Am/E
Cm/E♭
3fr
D7
Gm7
If I can find the sun in your eyes.
C7
F
C7
Some - times I love you,
F
C7
F
Some - times I hate you, But when I

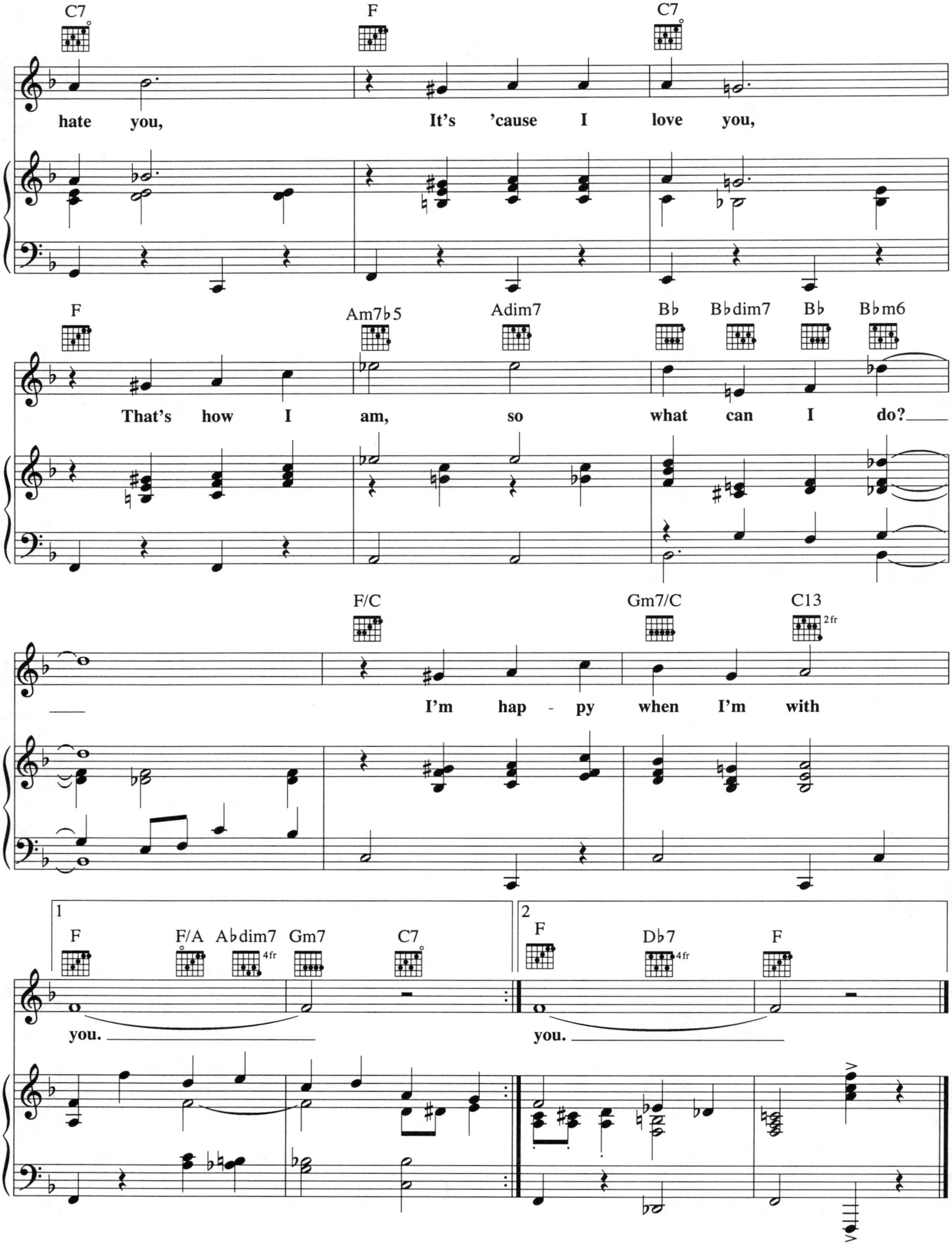
C7 F C7
hate you, It's 'cause I love you,
F Am7♭5 Adim7 B♭ B♭dim7 B♭ B♭m6
That's how I am, so what can I do?
F/C Gm7/C C13
I'm hap - py when I'm with
1
F F/A A♭dim7 Gm7 C7
you.
2
F D♭7 F
you.
2fr
4fr

SWEET SUE-JUST YOU

from RHYTHM PARADE

Words by WILL J. HARRIS
Music by VICTOR YOUNG

Moderately

Am7
D7
Am7
And the moon up high
Knows the rea - son why
D7
D7-9
G6
D7-9
G6
Sweet Sue,
it's you
D
Dm7
G7
No one else it seems
Ev - er
Bm7-5
E7
Am
Am/G#
shares my dreams
And with - out you, dear, I

Am7
Am7-5
D7
don't know what I'd do, In this
Am7
D7
Am7
heart of mine You live all the time
D7
D7-9
G6
C9
Sweet Sue, just
1
G6
Am7
D7
you. Ev - 'ry
2
G
C
Cm6
Gmaj7
you.
8va

STEPPIN' OUT WITH MY BABY

from the Motion Picture Irving Berlin's EASTER PARADE

Words and Music by
IRVING BERLIN

C/E
G7
Cmaj7
C6
C/E
G7
Cmaj7
C6
I won't waste your time. But if you should ask me
Gm7
C9
F6
A9
Dm
Dm/C
why I feel sub - lime, I'm step - pin' out
mf
Gm/B♭
A7
Dm
Dm/C
Gm/B♭
A7
Dm
Dm/C
with my ba - by. Can't go wrong 'cause I'm in right. It's for sure,
Gm/B♭
Em7♭5
Dm
Dm/F
Gm6
G♯dim7
A7
Dm6
not for may - be, that I'm all dressed up to - night.

Dm
Dm/C
Gm/B♭
A7
Dm
Dm/C
Step - pin' out ___ with my hon - ey, can't be bad ___ to
Gm/B♭
A7
Dm
Dm/C
Gm/B♭
Em7♭5
feel so good. _ Nev - er felt ___ quite so sun - ny.
Dm
Dm/F
Gm6
G#dim7
A7
Dm6
D6
Dmaj7
And I keep on knock - in' wood, _ there'll be smooth sail - in' 'cause
D
Dmaj7
D6
Dmaj7
I'm trim - min' my sails. ___
In my
(Girls Version) With a

D6
Dmaj7
D6
Dmaj7
D6
Em7/A
A7
Em7
A7
top hat and my white tie and my tails
bright shine on my shoes and on my nails
Dm
Dm/C
Gm/B♭
A7
Dm
Dm/C
step - pin' out with my ba - by, can't go wrong 'cause
Gm/B♭
A7
Dm
Dm/C
Gm/B♭
Em7♭5
I'm in right. Ask me when will the day be,
D/F♯
Fdim7
1
Em7
E♭7
D6
2
Em7
E♭7
D6
D6/9
the big day may be to - night. be to - night.

STOMPIN' AT THE SAVOY

Words and Music by BENNY GOODMAN, EDGAR SAMPSON,
CHICK WEBB and ANDY RAZAF

Gm7
C9
F
F7
so soft and close to mine, di - vine!
Bb7
B7
Bb7
Eb9
Bbm7-5
Eb9
Ab7
A7
How my heart is sing - in' While the band is swing-in'! Nev-er tired of
Ab7
Db7
C7
C9
F
rom - in' And stomp-in' with you at the Sa-voy. What joy! A per-fect hol - i - day!
C9
F
F#dim
Gm7
Sa - voy, where we can glide and sway; Sa - voy, there let me stomp a - way
C9
F
C9
F
Eb9-5
Fmaj9
with you. Sa - voy,

A STRING OF PEARLS

from THE GLENN MILLER STORY

Words by EDDIE DE LANGE
Music by JERRY GRAY

Ab+ Ab6 Ab7 Abmaj7 Ab Abmaj7 Ab7 Ab6 Ab+
wrapped in dreams and filled with love That old string
I've got some - thing just else for you. It's a string
8va bassa
Ab Bb9 Eb7 Ab Bb7
of pearls a - la Wool - worth.
of kiss - es for ba - by.
loco
Eb Ebmaj7 Eb7 Eb6 Eb+ Eb Eb+ Eb6 Eb7
'Til that hap - py day in Spring when you I buy
I found a love so sub - lime, right in that
Ebmaj7 Eb Ebmaj7 Eb7 Eb6 Eb+ Eb F9 Bb7
the wed-ding ring, Please A String Of Pearls a - la
old five and dime, with A String Of Pearls a - la
1 Eb6 Bb7 2 Eb6 D6 Eb6
Wool - worth. Wool - worth.
Wool - worth. Wool - worth.
ff

SWEET AND LOVELY

Words and Music by GUS ARNHEIM,
CHARLES N. DANIELS and HARRY TOBIAS

G♯dim7
E+
E7
Am/C
E/B
Am
A7
A7/E
E♭7♭5
noth-ing can com-pare to the sweet-ness of the one and on-ly one I
Am7/D
D7
D7
Am7/D
love.
Sweet and love-ly,
D7
Am7/D
D7
G9
Cmaj9
C6
7 fr
Cm6
2 fr
Sweet-er than the ros-es in May,
Sweet and love-ly,
D/A
A7sus
A7
D6
D7
Heav-en must have sent her my way.
Skies a-

Am7/D
D7
Am7/D
D7
bove me
nev - er were as blue as her eyes, ___
G9
Cmaj9
C6
7 fr
Cm6
2 fr
D/A
A7sus
A7
And she loves me,
Who would want a sweet - er sur - prise. _
D6
C9
D
When she nes - tles in my arms so ten - der - ly ___
sfz
C9
D6
D7
E♭9
there's a thrill that words can - not ex - press.
In my heart a song of love is
sfz
sfz

F
F7
B♭9
A7♯5
taunt - ing me,
Mel - o - dy
haunt - ing me.
D7
Am7/D
D7
Sweet
and
love - ly,
Sweet - er than the ros - es in May,
Am7/D
D7
G9
Cmaj9
C6
7 fr
Cm6
2 fr
And
she
loves
me,
D/A
A7sus
A7
1
D6
A7♯5
2
D6
There is noth - ing more I can say.

T'AIN'T WHAT YOU DO
(IT'S THE WAY THAT CHA DO IT)

Words and Music by SY OLIVER
and JAMES YOUNG

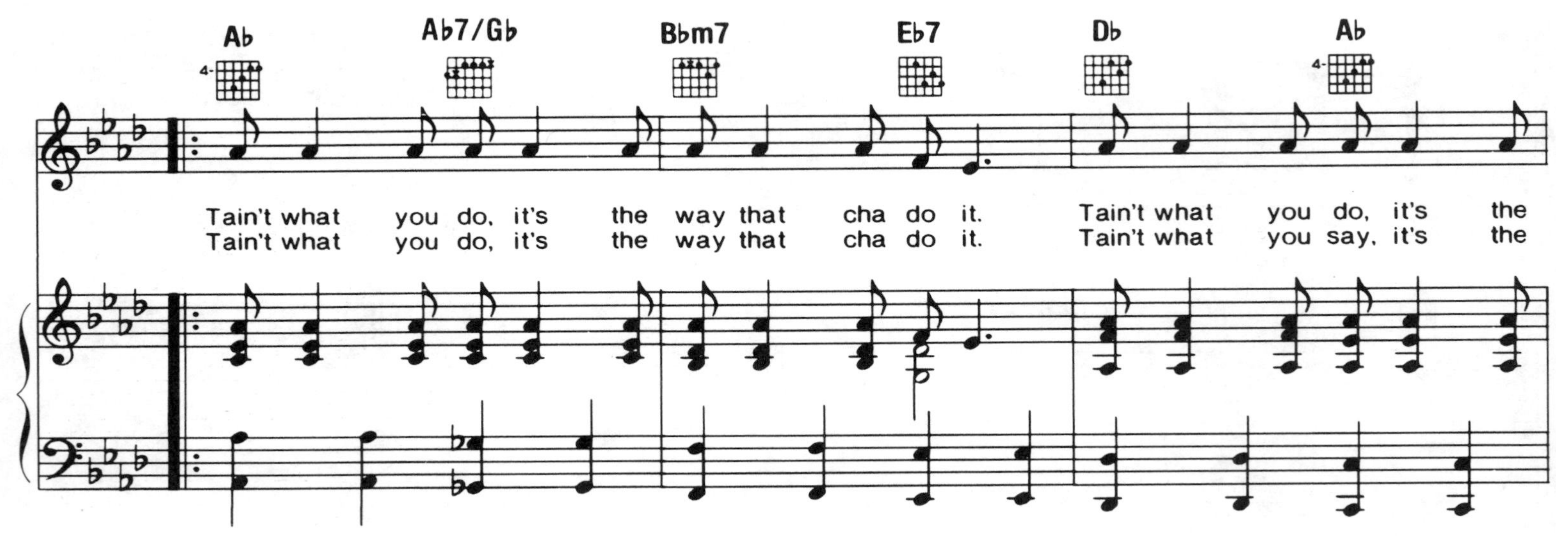

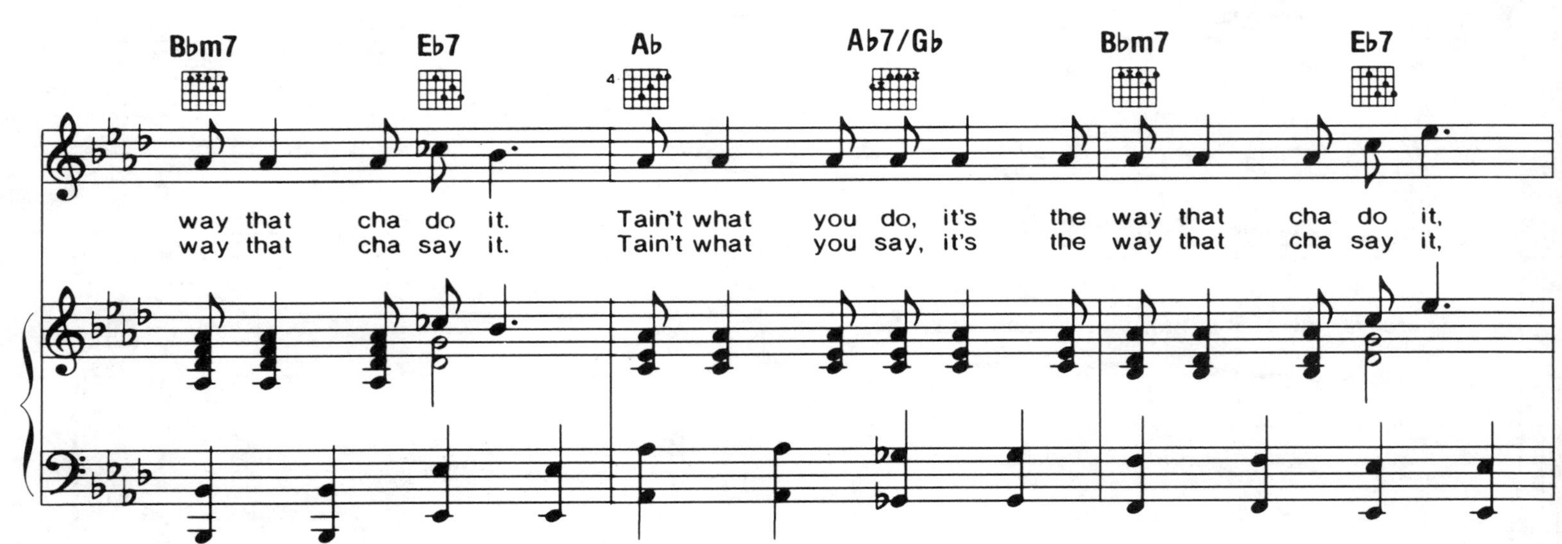

Ab Adim Bbm Eb7 Ab Adim Bbm Eb7 Ab Ab7/Gb
that's what gets _ re - sults. _ Tain't what you do, it's the
that's what gets _ re - sults. _ Tain't what you croon it's the
Bbm7 Eb7 Db Ab Bbm7 Eb7
time that cha do it. Tain't what you do it's the time that cha do it.
way that cha croon it. Tain't what you croon it's the way that cha croon it.
Ab Ab7/Gb Bbm7 Eb7 Ab Adim Bbm Eb7 Ab Ab7
Tain't what you do, it's the time that cha do it, That's what gets _ re - sults _ You can
Tain't what you croon it's the way that cha croon it, That's what gets _ re - sults _ If you're
Db6 Ebm7 Db9 Db6 Eb9 Ab
Guitar Tacet
try hard, _ don't mean a thing. _
lone - some _ and on the shelf. _

Ab
Ab7
Db6
Ebm7
Edim
Db6
Ab
Adim
Take it ea - sy
then your jive will swing.
It's your own fault
so just blame your-self.
Eb7
E9
Eb9
Ab
Ab7
Bbm7
Eb7
Tain't what you do, it's the place that cha do it.
Tain't what you say, it's the place that cha say it.
Db
Ab
Bbm7
Eb7
Ab
Ab7
Tain't what you do, it's the time that cha do it.
Tain't what you croon it's the time that cha croon it.
Tain't what you do, it's the
Tain't what you do, it's the
Bbm7
Eb7
Ab
Adim
Bbm7
Eb7
Ab
Adim
Bbm7
Eb7
Ab
Eb7
Ab
way that cha do it, that's what gets re - sults.
way that cha do it. that's what gets re - sults.

TAKE THE "A" TRAIN

Words and Music by
BILLY STRAYHORN

B♭m7
E♭7
A♭
to take a lit - tle ride a - round the cit - y.
B♭9♯11
Brook - lyn or Broad - way train,
B♭m7
E♭7
you'll see that old New York is might - y
A♭
A♭9
D♭
pret - ty. Take your ba - by sub - way

B♭7
rid - ing.
That's where
ro-mance may be
B♭m7
E♭9
E♭7♭9
A♭
hid - ing.
For - get
your car or
B♭9♯11
B♭m7
E♭7
air-plane.
You'll
find that it -'ll pay to take the
1
A♭
"A" train.
2 A♭
"A" train.

TANGERINE

from the Paramount Picture THE FLEET'S IN

Words by JOHNNY MERCER
Music by VICTOR SCHERTZINGER

A/E
Bm
E7
Em7/A
A7
D7#5
treme, wait till you see her face. Tan - ge -
Gm7
3fr
C7
F6
rine, she is all they claim,
F6/A
A♭dim7
4fr
Gm7
3fr
C7
Gm7
3fr
C7
with her eyes of night and lips as bright as
F
D7#5
Gm7
3fr
flame. Tan - ge - rine,

C7
F6
E7
when she danc - es by
Señ - or -
A
F♯m7
Bm7
2 fr
E7
A7
i - tas stare and ca - bal - le - ros sigh.
D7
D7♯5
Gm7
3 fr
C7
F6
And I've seen
toasts to Tan - ge - rine
F6/A
A♭dim7
4 fr
Gm7
3 fr
C7
Gm7
3 fr
C7
raised in ev - 'ry bar a - cross the Ar - gen -

A7
D7
D7#5
D7
Gm
3 fr
Gm/F
tine.
Yes, she has them all on the
Em7
A7
Dm7
F/G
G7
run but her heart be - longs to just one. Her
B♭
Gm7
3 fr
Gm7/C
C7
1
F
Cm/E♭
3 fr
heart be - longs to Tan - ge - rine.
D7
D7#5
2
F
Tan - ge - rine.
rit.

THAT OLD BLACK MAGIC

from the Paramount Picture STAR SPANGLED RHYTHM

Words by JOHNNY MERCER
Music by HAROLD ARLEN

i - cy fin - gers up and down my spine. The
Bb9#5/Eb
4fr
Eb6
Bb9#5
same old witch - craft when your eyes meet mine. The
Eb
3fr
same old tin - gle that I feel in - side,
cresc. poco a poco
Db
Db7
4fr
and then that el - e - va - tor starts its ride,
rit.
f a tempo

Ab6
3 fr
Abm6
4 fr
Ebmaj9
and down and down I go, 'round and 'round
dim. poco a poco
C+
Fm7
Emaj7
Eb
3 fr
3
I go like a leaf that's caught in the tide.
p
Cm
3 fr
Ab9#11
3
I should stay a - way but what can I do?
mf
G9
C9
I hear your name and I'm a - flame,

Fm
a - flame with such a burn - ing de -
D♭9
A♭m6
sire that on - ly your kiss
B♭13
can put out the fire. For
E♭
you're the lov - er I have wait - ed for,
pp
p

B♭m7/E♭
6fr
the mate that fate had me cre -
cresc. poco a poco
E♭9
A♭
4fr
at - ed for, and ev - 'ry time
f
A♭m6
4fr
your lips meet mine, dar - ling,
A♭6/9
A♭m6
4fr
E♭maj7
3fr
down and down I go, 'round and 'round
dim.
p

C+
Fm7/E♭
3
I go in a spin, loving the
Fm7♭5/E♭
6fr
B♭7sus/E♭
spin I'm in, under that old black mag-
rit.
1
E♭6
2
-ic called love! That love!
a tempo
Fm7♭5/E♭
E♭6/9
rit. e dim.
pp

THERE'LL BE SOME CHANGES MADE

from ALL THAT JAZZ

Words by BILLY HIGGINS
Music by W. BENTON OVERSTREET

C7
F7
F+
You're here to - day and then to - mor - row you're gone,
'Cause they are cer - tain - ly not suit - ed for me,
B♭
Gm
C7
F7
I loved a man for man - y years gone by,
There was a time when I thought that way,
B♭7
B♭+
E♭
I tho't his love for me would nev - er die,
That's why I'm all a - lone here to - day
C7
F
A7
D7
He made some chang - es that would nev - er do
Since ev - 'ry - one these days seeks some - thing new
From now
From now

Gm
Gdim
C7
F7
F7sus
F7
on I'm goin' to make some chang - es too.
on I'm goin' to seek some new things too.
For there's a
G9
change in the weath - er There's a change in the sea
C9
So from now on there'll be a change in me,
My
D7
G7
walk will be dif - f'rent my talk and my name

C9
C7
F7
Noth - in' a - bout me is goin' to be the same, I'm goin' to
G7
change my way of liv - in' if that ain't e - nough,
C9
Then I'll change the way that I Strut my stuff, 'cause
D7
G7
no - bod - y wants you when you're old and gray

C9
F7
B♭
A♭7
G7
There'll be some chang - es made to - day
There'll be some chang - es
G9
made. For there's a change in the fash - ions, Ask the
fem - i-nine folks
Ev - en Jack Ben - ny has been
D7
chang - ing jokes,
I must make some chang - es from

G7
C9
old to the new
I must do things just the same as
C7
F7
G7
oth - ers do,
I'm goin' to change my long, tall
'Mam - ma
Dad - dy
for a
C9
lit - tle short Fat,
Goin' to change the num - ber where
D7
I live at.
I must have some lov - in' or I'll

Additional Choruses

1. There's a change in your manner
   And a change in your way
   There was time once when you was O.K.
   You once said you saved ev'ry kiss for my sake
   Now you're giving all the girls an even break
   I'm gonna send out invitations to the men I know
   'Cause you're gettin' colder than an Eskimo
   I must have my lovin' or I'll fade away
   There'll be some changes made to-day
   There'll be some changes made.

2. For there's a change in your manner
   There's a change in your style
   And here of late you never wear a smile
   You don't seem to act like a real lover should
   You can't thrill your mamma if you're made of wood
   I gotta have a man who loves me like a real live Skeik
   With a tasty kiss that lingers for a week
   I'm not over sixty so it's time to say
   There'll be some changes made to-day
   There'll be some changes made.

3. For there's a change in your squeezin'
   There's a change in your kiss
   It used to have a kick that I now miss
   You'd set me on fire when you used to tease
   Now each time you call I just sit there and freeze
   You had a way of making love that made a hit with me
   One time you could thrill me but it's plain to see
   You're not so ambitious as you used to be
   There'll be some changes made by me
   There'll be some changes made.

4. There's a change in the weather
   There's a change in the sea
   From now on there'll be a change in me
   I'm tired of working all of my life
   I'm gonna grab a rich husband and be his wife
   I'm going to ride around in a big limousine
   Wear fancy clothes and put on plenty of steam
   No more tired puppies, will I treat you mean
   There'll be some changes made to-day
   There'll be some changes made.

5. For there's a change in your manner
   There's a change in your smile
   From now on you can't be worth my while
   I'm right here to tell you with you I'm thru
   Your brand of lovin' will never do
   I'm gettin' tired of eating just butter and bread
   I could enjoy a few pork chops instead
   You know variety is the spice of life they say
   There'll be some changes made to-day (I'll get mine)
   There'll be some changes made.

Additional Choruses by WILSON and RINGLE

WOODCHOPPER'S BALL

By JOE BISHOP
and WOODY HERMAN

Dm7
Dm7/G
C6
F7
C

Dm
G7
C6
C
F7
C
Dm
G7
C
C6

TUXEDO JUNCTION

Words by BUDDY FEYNE
Music by ERSKINE HAWKINS, WILLIAM JOHNSON and JULIAN DASH

B♭
E♭7
F7
B♭
South, in Bir - ming - ham, I mean South in Al -
mf
E♭7
F7
B♭
E♭
Edim
- a - bam's an old place where peo - ple go to dance
B♭
F7
B♭
F7
B♭
the night a - way. They all drive or walk
E♭7
F7
B♭
E♭7
F7
for miles to get jive that South - ern style, s - low

B♭
E♭
Edim
B♭
F7
jive that makes you want to dance 'til break of day.
B♭
B♭9
E♭
E♭7
It's a junc - tion where the
B♭
E♭7
B♭7
E♭
town folks meet. At each func - tion,
E♭7
B♭
Cm7
F7
In their tux they greet you. Come on
ff

B♭
E♭7
F7
down, for - get your care. Come on
down you'll find me there. So long
E♭
Edim
town! I'm head - in' for Tux - e -
do Junc - tion now. Way down
1 B♭
2 B♭
fz

WHEN I TAKE MY SUGAR TO TEA

from the Paramount Picture MONKEY BUSINESS

Words and Music by SAMMY FAIN, IRVING KAHAL and PIERRE NORMAN

Gmi.7
C+
F
Gmi.7
C7
D♭7
C7
F
on the cor - ner, For the moon in lov - er's lane;
C
G7
C7
I'm do - ing things I nev - er did be - fore:
REFRAIN
F
Cdim.
C7
F
Cdim.
p - mf
When I take my su - gar to tea, All the boys are jeal - ous of
C7
D7
Gmi.7
B♭mi.
me; 'Cause I nev - er take her where the gang goes, When I

F
C7
F
B♭
F
C
F
Cdim.
C7
take my sug-ar to tea. I'm a row-dy dow-dy, that's me, She's a
F
Cdim.
C7
D7
high-hat ba-by, That's she. So I nev-er take her where the
Gmi.7
B♭mi.
F
C7
F
F7
Cdim.
B♭
gang goes, When I take my sug-ar to tea. Ev-'ry Sun-day
E♭7
af-ter-noon, We for-get a-bout our cares,

F
G7
D♭7
Rub - bing el - bows at the Ritz
With those mil - lion -
C7
Cdim.
C7
F
Cdim.
C7
aires. When I take my sug - ar to tea, I'm as
F
Cdim.
C7
D7
Ritz - y as I can be, 'Cause I nev - er take her where the
Gmi.7
B♭mi.
F
C7
1. F
B♭
F
C7
2. F
gang goes, When I take my sug - ar to tea. When I tea.

WHEN THE SUN COMES OUT

Lyric by TED KOEHLER
Music by HAROLD ARLEN

Dm7
G7#5
F7
E♭dim
Dm7
G7#5
like they did be - fore that ol' storm broke out. And my
F7
F#dim
G7
Gm7
C7♭9
man / gal walked off and left me in the rain. Though he's / she's gone, I
F
Fm
C
C#dim
Dm7
G7#5
doubt if he'll / she'll stay a - way for good, I'd stop liv - in' if he / she should. Love is
Cmaj7
C
Cdim
Gm
fun - ny; it's not al - ways peach-es, cream and hon - ey.

A7#5
A7
Dm7
F
C
F
Just when ev - 'ry - thing looked bright and sun - ny, sud - den - ly the cy - clone
Dm7
G7
Dm7
G7#5
F7
E♭dim
came. I'll nev - er be the same 'til that sun comes
Dm7
G7#5
F7
F#dim
G7
out and the rain stops beat - in' on my win - dow pane. If my
Gm7
C7♭9
F
Fm
C
C#dim
heart holds out, let it rain and let it pour, it may

Dm7
G7#5
C
E9
not be long be - fore there's a knock - in' at my door. Then you'll
Am7
Fm
E7#5
E7
A7
D7♭5
Dm7
G7♭9
know the one I loved walked in, when the sun comes
1 C
Am7
Dm7
G7#5
C
Am7
out.
Dm7
G7#5
2 C
F9
C
When the out.

YOU BROUGHT A NEW KIND OF LOVE TO ME

from the Paramount Picture THE BIG POND

Words and Music by SAMMY FAIN, IRVING KAHAL and PIERRE NORMAN

A♭7
4fr
D♭/A♭
4fr
D♭m/A♭
4fr
Never will I meet one sweeter than
3
A♭
4fr
you. Would you
A♭+
Fm6/A♭
6fr
Fm6
turn away or could you really learn to
B♭7
B♭7♭9
B♭7
care If I'd ever dare to say, "I love

Eb7
Eb7sus
Eb7
Bbm7
you."
If the night-in - gales could
rit.
p - mf a tempo
Eb7
Ab
Ab7
G7
Gb7
4fr
sing like you
They'd sing much sweet - er than they do
For
Bb7
Eb7sus
Eb7
Ab
you've brought a new kind of love to me.
mf
Eb7sus
Eb7
Bbm7
Eb7
If the sand-man brought me dreams of you
I'd

Ab
Ab7
G7
Gb7
F7
Bb7
want to sleep my whole life thru, For you've brought a new kind of
Eb7sus
Eb7
Ab
Dbm
Ab
no chord
love to me. I know that
Fm
C/E
Ab7/Eb
Bb7/D
Db7
C7
I'm the slave, you're the queen, But still you can un - der -
mf
Fm
Eb
Bb+
Fdim
stand That un - der - neath it all you're a maid

B♭7
E♭7
B♭m7
And I am on - ly a man. I would work and slave _ the
E♭7
A♭
A♭7
G7
G♭7
F7
whole day thru, _ If I could hur - ry home to you, _ For
B♭7
E♭7sus
E♭7
1.
A♭
Adim7
you've brought a new kind of love to me.
poco rit.
a tempo
E♭7
2.
A♭
D♭m
A♭
If the me.

YOU TOOK ADVANTAGE OF ME

from PRESENT ARMS

Words by LORENZ HART
Music by RICHARD RODGERS

Ab
Eb7
Ab
Eb7#5
Ab
B7
Bb7
Eb
ton - ic before you gave me "that!" A
broth- er and so I loved my horse. But
Bbm7
Eb
Bbm7
Eb
Bbm7
Eb
Eb7#5
Ab
D7
men - tal de - fi - cient you'll grade me, I've giv - en you plen - ty of
hors - es are fre-quent - ly sil - ly, Mine ran from the beach of Ka -
Gm
C
C7#5
da - ta. You came, you saw and you
lu - a, And left me a - lone for a
F9b5
Eb/Bb
Bm6
Bb7
slayed me, And that - a is that - a!
fil - ly, so I - a picked you - a!

Eb
3fr
Edim7
Bb7/F
Bb7
I'm a sent - i - men - tal sap, that's all.
Eb/G
3fr
Gbdim7
Fm7
Bb7
What's the use of try - ing not to fall? I
Eb
3fr
Eb7
Ab
4fr
Fm7b5
Eb/Bb
6fr
Eb+/Bb
Fm7/Bb
Bb7
have no will, you've made your kill 'cause you took ad - van-tage of
Eb
3fr
B7
Bb7
Eb
3fr
Edim7
Bb7/F
Bb7
me! I'm just like an ap - ple on a bough

Eb/G Gbdim7 Fm7 Bb7 Eb Eb7
And you're gon - na shake me down some - how, so what's the use, you've
Ab Fm7b5 Eb/Bb Eb+/Bb Fm7/Bb Bb7 Eb Gm/D
cooked my goose 'cause you took ad - van - tage of me!
Cm D7 G7 C7 F7 Bb7
I'm so hot and both-ered that I don't know my el - bow from my
Eb Cm D7 G7 C7
ear; I suf - fer some-thing aw - ful each time you go And

F7 Bb7 Gm7 Fm7 Bb7 Eb Edim7
3fr 3fr
much worse when _ you're near. Here am I with all my
Bb7/F Bb7 Eb/G Gbdim7
3fr
bridg - es burned, _ just a babe in arms where
Fm7 Bb7 Eb Eb7 Ab Fm7b5
3fr 4fr
you're con - cerned, _ so lock the doors _ and call me yours _ 'cause you
Eb/Bb Eb+/Bb Fm7/Bb Bb7
6fr
took ad - van - tage of
1
Eb Ab6 Bb7
3fr 3fr
me!
2
Eb
3fr
me!

YOU TURNED THE TABLES ON ME

Words by SIDNEY MITCHELL
Music by LOUIS ALTER

D9
4fr
G7
C9
F6/A
A♭m6
Gm6
D7/F♯
prompt me to say: You turned the ta-bles on me,
Gm7
C7
C+
Fmaj7
F6
F+
F
And now I'm fall - ing for you.
You turned the ta - bles on me.
I can't be - lieve that it's true.
I al - ways
F7
B♭
B♭m
thought when you brought the love - ly pre-sents you bought why had-n't you brought me more,

G♯dim7
Gm7
G♯dim7
But now if you'd come I'd wel-come an-y-thing from the five
F
D7
D♭9
C7
F6/A
A♭m6
Gm6
D7/F♯
and ten cent store. You used to call me the top,
Gm7
C7
C+
Fmaj7
F6
F+
F
F7
D♭m6
Cm6
2fr
You put me up on a throne.
You let me fall with a drop
Bdim7
Cm
3fr
Cm/F
5fr
F7♭9
B♭maj9
B♭6
and now I'm out on my own.

B♭m6
But af - ter think - ing it o - ver and o - ver,
F
G7
F6/A
A♭m6
I got what was com - ing to me,
Just like the sting of a bee,
Gm6 Gm7
C7
F
G7
C9
F/A
A♭m6 Gm6
you turned the ta - bles on me.
You turned the ta - bles on me,
F
B♭7
F6

YOU'D BE SO NICE TO COME HOME TO

from SOMETHING TO SHOUT ABOUT

Words and Music by
COLE PORTER

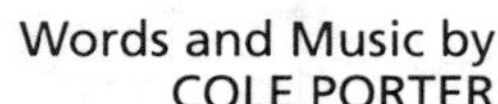

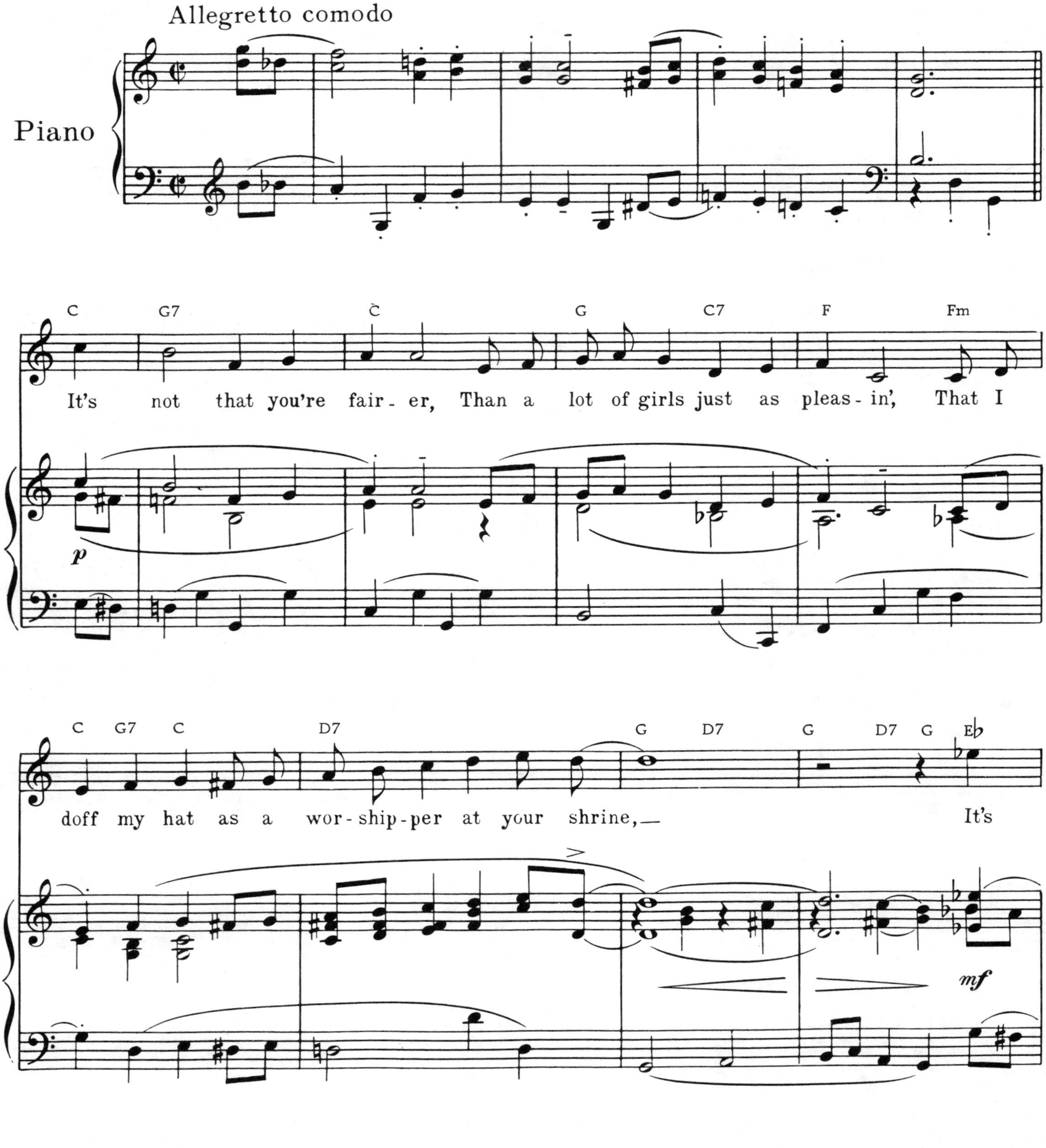

Allegretto comodo
Piano
C G7 C G C7 F Fm
It's not that you're fair - er, Than a lot of girls just as pleas - in', That I
p
C G7 C D7 G D7 G D7 G E♭
doff my hat as a wor - ship - per at your shrine, — It's
mf

B♭7
E♭
B♭
E♭7
A♭
not that you're rar-er Than as-par-a-gus out of sea-son, No, my
B♮
E♭
Cm6
E♭dim.
E♭
Fdim.
D7
G
dar-ling, this is the reas-on Why you've got to be mine:
rit.
p
mf
F
E7
Am
Refrain (rather slow with feeling)
ten.
ten.
Dm6
E7
Am
E7
You'd be so nice to come home to,
p - mf a tempo
Am
C7
F
C+
You'd be so nice by the fire,

F
Am
Dm7
B7(♭5)
E7
While the breeze, on high, sang a
D dim.
Am
G7
Am6
F7
B7
lull - a - by, You'd be all that I could de -
mf
E
B7
E
D
E7
Am
Dm6
E7
sire, Un - der stars, chilled by the
p
Am
E7
Am
C7
3
win - ter, Un - der an Aug - ust moon,
cresc.

F
C+
F
A
Dm
Burn - ing a - bove,
You'd be
C dim.
C
F
Fm6
so
nice, You'd be par - a - dise to come
cresc.
mf espr.
1. C
Ab7
D7
G7
C
F
E7
home to
and
love.
You'd be
f
mf
2. C
Ab7
D7
G7
C
home to
and
love.
f espr.
p

YOU'RE THE CREAM IN MY COFFEE
from HOLD EVERYTHING

Words and Music by B.G. DeSYLVA,
LEW BROWN and RAY HENDERSON

Eb9
Ab6
Ab7+5
Ab6
love - tales And each phrase dove - tails
sav - or Bring out its fla - vor
F13
Fm7
F7-5
You've heard each known way This way is
So this is clear, dear, You're my Wor -
Bb7-9
Bb9sus
Bb7+5
Eb6/9
Eb
Ebmaj9
Ebdim
my own way You're the sail of my love - boat
cester - shire, dear,
Fm6
Bb7
Fm6
Bb7
Fm6
Bb7
You're the cap - tain and crew. You will al - ways be
Fm6
Bb7
1 Eb
D7
Bb7
2 Eb
my ne - ces - si - ty I'd be lost with - out you. you.
f

YOU'RE NOBODY 'TIL SOMEBODY LOVES YOU

Words and Music by RUSS MORGAN,
LARRY STOCK and JAMES CAVANAUGH

Am D7 G6 D7♯5
no - bod - y 'til some - bod - y cares. You
Bm7 B♭dim Am7
may be king, you may pos - sess the world and it's gold, but
A6/9 A9♯5 A9 Am7 D7 Am7 D7 D7♯5
gold won't bring you hap - pi - ness when you're grow - ing old. The
G B7 E7♭9 E7 B7/F♯ E7/G♯
world still is the same, you'll nev - er change it, as

Am
E7
Am
E7/B
sure as the stars shine a - bove.
Am/C
C
C#dim7
You're no - bod - y 'til some - bod - y loves
G
E7
Am
E7/B
Am/C
A7
D7
you, so find your - self some - bod - y to
R.H.
1
G
F13sus
F9
Eb7sus
Eb7
D9
4fr
love. You're
2
G
Cm7
3fr
G6
love.
L.H.